After six years of serving a congregation as Mahan's colleague, when he retired I challenged him to share with current pastors from his experience. He took up the challenge. From his continued work with clergy we have in these re-frames the gift of his wisdom to all of us who remain in the trenches of pastoral leadership.

Nancy E. Petty, Pastor
Pullen Memorial Baptist Church
Raleigh, North Carolina

Mahan Siler's relational theology and covenantal practices are beautifully expressed in these letters. His curiosity evokes yours. His self-awareness invites your own internal work. His confidence in pastoral leaders, which the reader feels throughout the book, is placed in you for a purpose. The vocation's relational stance is crucial for our time when separation dominates.

Daniel Pryfogle
Theologian and entrepreneur, cofounder and CEO of Sympara

Mahan Siler offers fresh words and hopeful reflections on the life and calling of the pastor by sharing moments from his own story. Mahan is a wise voice in our Baptist tradition and beyond. His ability to describe the innovative, creative, and Spirit-filled work of the pastor and church is encouraging and makes this a treasured book for everyone.

Leah Grundset Davis, Pastor
Ravensworth Baptist Church
Annandale, Virginia

Mahan Siler

Letters
to Nancy
Re-frames that Mattered

© 2020
Published in the United States by Nurturing Faith Inc., Macon GA,
www.nurturingfaith.net.

Library of Congress Cataloging-in-Publication Data is available.

ISBN: 978-1-63528-104-0

Dedication

Wayne E. Oates

Contents

Acknowledgments

These acknowledgments are expressions of gratitude. Writing is a solitary endeavor, but we do not write alone. This book has been created in community.

Present to me in this writing have been mentor John R. Claypool and teacher Wayne E. Oates, to whom this book is dedicated. As assistant to John Claypool, I experienced with him the ambiguities and wonders embedded in pastoral ministry. Wayne Oates, by unpacking a pastoral situation in a class one day, elicited from me a surprising "Yes, I want to do that!" And I have, both as pastor and my work with pastors. Later, Dr. Oates was my major professor in doctoral studies, which for him included a friendship for life.

This community includes Dan Synder and Guy Sayles, who engaged these reframes from the idea stage to rough draft to manuscript to book. Their wisdom and support were indispensable. And Guy further graced this book by writing the foreword.

Carol Majors was an early advocate. She gave oversight to my website that included earlier entries of "Reframes That Mattered," the basis of this book.

With a book addressed to pastors, I am indebted to active pastors who read the manuscript. Like no one else, they could critique from their pastoral experiences. These pastors include Nancy Sehested, Mary Apicella, Daniel Pryfogile, Steve Hyde, Leah Grundset Davis, Jim Chatham, Missy Harris, Paula Dempsey, Kim Buchanan, and friends Cannan Hyde and Richard Hester, a former professor of pastoral theology. This gratitude includes over fifty clergy who participated in the AnamCara collegial clergy communities from 2000 to 2015. The ideas in this book have been field-tested with them. And there is Larry Matthews. Larry was a near-by pastor and friend who introduced me to systems thinking.

Nancy Petty, the current senior pastor of Pullen Memorial Baptist Church, inspired this writing with her initial challenge: "Mahan, write something practical, something useful for us back here 'in the trenches.'" From our earlier experience as colleagues is the gift of an ongoing friendship that continues to nurture and delight.

I am also indebted to two editors, Ulrike Guthrie and Catherine Reid, who helped with style and structure. And my grandson Walton has provided the technical assistance that preserved my sanity.

The Alliance of Baptists with Nurturing Faith Publishing has made this book possible. I am thankful and indebted to this partnership.

Finally, the community of support includes my family, in particular my wife, Janice. Her respect for my vocation and my writing amazes me with its constancy. My deepest gratitude is for her.

Within it all I give thanks to God, the Music that wants to sound though these human words.

Foreword

Guy Sayles

I'm graced and grateful to know and be known by my friend Mahan Siler. He has given me innumerable gifts: a warm and hospitable welcome, realistic and hopeful encouragement, and unconditional and truthful love. He has listened to me with a receptivity that has made it possible for me to clarify my feelings and to give voice to them. Mahan has asked me countless questions—provocative, sometimes confounding, but finally clarifying questions. He has freely and generously offered me gleanings from his storehouse of hard-earned wisdom, but he has never done so with condescension or the put-on airs of an "expert."

All of these qualities which I so respect in Mahan Siler are evident in this wonderful book. We hear sounding through it the insights from his wide reading, his thoughtful pondering, and his reflective practice as a pastor, a pastoral counselor, and an educator of both pastors and therapists. These words express Mahan's abiding commitment to local faith communities, where people tell the stories and perform the rituals which enliven and sustain them and where they discern, in the give-and-take of genuine conversation, their responses to the nearness of God's Beloved Community.

We're listening here to the voice of an engaged and still-growing elder as he talks with us about what it means to be a congregational leader and about how to serve faithfully and sustainably in that role. Central to the book and at the heart of Mahan's understanding of this vocation is a conviction that being a congregational leader is far more than a job; it is a way among other ways of becoming more fully who we are, pursuing our wholeness, and "working out our salvation." He trusts that ministry can be a means of transformation for ministers and for those whom they serve.

Mahan uses his own experiences of growth and development as case studies from which the rest of us may learn. He writes about them as "reframes"; he recounts what his perspectives and practices had been and what—in response to a variety of encounters with ideas, people, and systems—they became. His descriptions of these reframes seamlessly weave theory and practice, content and process, theology and spirituality. They exemplify Ken Wilber's invitation to "transcend and include"[1]—to move beyond where we have been but not to leave behind what remains valuable.

From time to time I teach leadership in seminary settings and coach pastors who are in the day-to-day crucible of guiding congregations. I'll be putting this book in their hands, and I hope they will let its wisdom seep into their hearts, spirits, and minds; shape their practices; and stimulate their ongoing transformation. It has done those things for me.

Note

[1] Ken Wilbur, *A Brief History of Everything*, second edition (Boston: Shambala, 2007), 43–44.

This is a contribution Wilbur makes to transpersonal psychology: each stage of development does not replace the previous stages, rather each stage transcends and includes the previous stages.

Tribute

To the chutzpah of pastors

The courage, week after week, to declare the gracious mystery of God with words that fall short every time,

the courage to stand with conviction, offering an alternative worldview of Shalom to the dominant culture of competitive, often violent ways of relating,

the courage to enter, upon invitation, into the private places of a person's life and be there with presence, faith, and sometimes insight,

the courage to call for trusting the Christ spirit that might take us where we do not wish to go,

the courage to be a flawed leader of an imperfect institution that frequently contradicts the compassion it declares,

and the courage to bear the symbols of God, even be a symbol of God, at the perilous risk of playing God.

Introduction

These letters are the fruit from a particular seed planted two decades ago.

It was August 1998. I had just retired as pastor of Pullen Memorial Baptist Church in Raleigh, North Carolina. For the last six years of those fifteen years, Nancy Petty and I were colleagues. Those six years of shared ministry, invigorating to us both, were seasoned with frequent conversations about pastoral ministry.

During the week following my final Sunday, I stopped by the church to pick up my mail. Nancy was in her office, sitting behind a desk strewn with pink slip reminders of phone calls to return. She challenged me, "Mahan, you say you want to write from your experiences as pastor. Well, write for us! Write something practical, something useful for us back here in 'the trenches.'"

I caught her on a frustrating day; she caught me in a teachable moment. For her, this was the first week of additional interim responsibilities. For me, this was the first week of a next chapter, a new freedom. I walked away pondering her request, which over time became a summons.

Over the next two decades, I have heeded her challenge. In the first decade, I gathered pastors into small groups of peer learning, support, and accountability. Three Lilly grants made them possible. In those years I worked with over sixty pastors of all denominations, including a few rabbis. These small communities I named AnamCara, Celtic for "soul friend." From these experiences came *AnamCara: Collegial Clergy Communities*, published in 2008.

In 2008 I began to post on my website short reflections on pastoral leadership. After ten years, I have returned to Nancy's specific challenge: to write something useful to pastors "in the trenches." I selected and polished some of these posted reflections and now offer them in this book in the form of letters.

These reflections are based on those times in my experience when one way to see our work—a *frame*—shifted to a different way to see pastoral ministry—a *reframe*. By seeing differently, I changed how I led. I'm told that Ted Williams, the infamous baseball slugger, offered this advice to a younger struggling ball player: "If you are in a slump, don't try harder. Change your stance!" That is the intention in these reframes. Each one altered my stance and the way I "swung." In these letters I call them "Reframes That Mattered."

I imagine these reframes being helpful in two ways. They may provide a different way of seeing your work. And they may provoke in you the same question they provoked in me: Which reframes have changed the way you offer ministry?

Nancy Petty, no longer a young pastor, continues to serve this same congregation. She is now the longest-serving pastor—as associate, co-pastor, and now senior minister—in the church's history. *Letters to Nancy* is addressed to her as a belated response to her initial request. But more than that, in this book "Nancy" has become any pastor. I'm writing to her with others of you in the trenches also in mind.

You have in your hand letters from a pastor from one generation writing to the next generations of clergy leaders of congregations. I am nearly eighty-four as I write this. I am among others my age who are late in waking up to our privileges as white, male, heterosexual Americans with economic security. Clearer now is the fact that I have lived in systems that advantage me while disadvantaging others. This limits what I see. While my privilege makes possible this writing, it's also true that my unacknowledged biases will surely show up in these letters. I'm counting on you, the reader, to both learn from me and as a counterpoint to me, to let my stances challenge yours, to allow what I see to clarify what you see.

If women clergy, African-American, Latinx, and non-American pastors, Roman Catholic priests, and rabbis find in these pages useful insights for their practice of ministry, I will be delighted. Even with all the differences that could be named between us, congregations are congregations are congregations. Leading local congregations is what we have in common.

We live our individual ways of being pastor. But we also live the life of our times. Our historical context is ever shaping the gifts we are called to offer and able to offer. When I began as a pastor, the life of the times was optimistic, a characteristic of early post-WWII years. The culture reflected predictability, stability, and likeness.

Not so with you. You serve within a culture of unpredictability, instability, and differences, often extreme, polarizing differences. During these past few decades, computer-based technology has become the principle organizer of life at a pace beyond our ability to absorb. Change, once at arithmetic speed (2-4-6-8-10-12), now increases at an exponential pace (2-4-8-16-32-64). Such a pace is breathtaking.

As a leader of congregations, you stand in that crucible, facing both ways, valuing both ministries—the grief work in letting go and the birthing of new life. You live the tension of people attempting to drink new wine in both old and new wine skins. You know this as well—that creative, imaginative, innovative change is more possible during times of disorder and uncertainty than when everything seems the same as it has been.

These letters, each one a reframe, are divided into three sections. The first section is one letter, titled "The Wager," a reframe that is so foundational that I place it by itself at the beginning.

The second section of sixteen reframes in letter form are efforts to stimulate reflection on some bread-and-butter aspects of our work. They invite insight— that is, "seeing into"—a different way. With each reframe I will include how a particular awareness changed the way I offered leadership. You can read these letters in any order. Each one stands on its own as a portal into some feature of pastoral leadership.

The third section focuses on the inner journey of our own transformation. I propose that personal and social transformation is the heart of ministry. This final section of the book reflects the paradox of transformation: becoming who we already are. This will include the practice of contemplative prayer and seeing our ministry as spiritual practice.

This book is a thank offering. I am thankful for a vocation that has given me a ringside seat on how people make meaning of their lives and, in the process, watch myself make meaning with them. Being a pastor was my way into these intimate, "take off your shoes" sacred places where Spirit is a felt presence. We pastors get to show up in these holy moments. This grace is the source of my gratitude.

Included in my thanksgiving is my gratitude for laity, especially lay leaders. While in these letters I will affirm the unique position of the pastor as leader in the congregational system, I no less value the role of lay leaders. Pastors and lay leaders, as if square dancing, sometimes lead, sometimes follow.

A farmer friend speaks of preserving the healthiest seeds from one harvest for the next planting. I consider these reframes to be my healthiest seeds. They are the best I have to offer to a vocation I love and to those who practice it.

Section I

The Wager

Dear Nancy,

From my perch, twenty years after retirement, I am astounded by the wager we make in faith and in ministry. You and I have this in common: we have bet our lives on a reality we cannot measure or control or prove or name precisely. This reality, in the words of Rudolf Otto, is *mysterium tremendum et fascinans*: *mystery* that makes us *tremble* with awe, yet ever lures us forward with *fascination*.[1]

Furthermore, you and I wager that this mystery, most clear to us in Jesus of Nazareth, is a Love from which nothing in life or death, now or later, can separate us. At its essence this reality is relational and interconnected, a force for us, not against or indifferent to us. It's a narrative with purpose, not a composite of random events "full of sound and fury signifying nothing."[2] And as if all of this is not wonder enough, this gracious mystery wants to be incarnated in us and in those we serve.

So strong was this fascination that you and I have staked our vocational lives on this imperceptible Spirit that, like the wind, blows where it wills. You go around declaring the invisibles: grace, love, forgiveness, beauty, communion, justice, wisdom, and integrity. We dare, each of us, to keep leaning into this unsolvable dilemma: that what we most care about cannot be captured with words. It takes a gambler's heart to go on this journey of faith.

Daily, you wager with your life energy. Daily, you place your bet with the coins of your time—thirty, forty, fifty, sixty, seventy hours a week; twenty, thirty, and for some people even fifty, sixty, seventy years of life—declaring a wager that can look foolish in a world that distrusts the immeasurable. You surrender. You show up. You doubt. You adore. You wonder. You stammer. Your "fingers point to the Moon,"[3] so you point. You witness. Day by day, Sunday by Sunday, week by week you risk words for this mystery of divine reality, knowing that they fall short every time.

This fact remains: Without the existence and experience of this mysterious Spirit, our vocation collapses into folly.

Will Campbell was a maverick Baptist in my time. Once, when I was in a group of pastors with Will, the conversation turned in an "ain't it awful" direction. Weary of our complaining, it seems, Will stopped our bitching session in its tracks. "Well, as I see it," he said in his Southern drawl, "life is a horse race. And I'm bettin' on Jesus." His few words pierced to the heart of our calling. No matter that we disagreed on how to interpret Jesus. What mattered—we all knew it—was we were bettin' on Jesus.

You are as well. You and I keep bettin' on Jesus, so much so that we serve the church that is called to be his body in the world. The wager, if we stop to consider it for a moment, is profoundly astonishing.

This reframe, a full-of-mystery wager stoked by radical amazement, surfaced with clarity for me against the backdrop of its opposite—the frame of my denomination's ideological turn toward certainty. In this frame the faithful are defined *in*; the others are defined *out*. "Right believing" became the measure.

Nancy, you too experienced this turn toward certainty with judgment. This radical shift occurred and reached its peak about the time you entered seminary. You know the story. In the late 1970s and early 1980s a fundamentalist arm of Southern Baptists gradually, strategically seized control of the denomination and established doctrinal norms for membership, the primary one being the infallibility of Scripture. Denominational agencies, including seminaries, were required to affirm doctrinal statements of faith. Like a knife, this set of beliefs divided those "in" from those "out," the loyal from the disloyal, truth from error. We felt the sharp edge of this knife, so much so that the denominational ties of Pullen, our congregation, were severed in 1992 shortly before you joined our staff.

This was my learning: Up close I saw the danger of religion that hardens its arteries in the form of set beliefs. Such hardening forfeits mystery, silences wonder. For right beliefs thrive on certainty fueled by binary thinking with its either/or, right/wrong, in/out, true/false ways of seeing. This way of thinking also needs enemies in order to thrive. Having enemies fuels the battle for preserving "truth" with sacrificial efforts.

During that fundamentalist takeover, a gift dropped into my lap. During my early years at Pullen, the book *Man Is Not Alone*, loaned to me by a church member, introduced me to the life and thought of Rabbi Joshua Abraham Heschel. That book and Heschel's other writings reawakened in me the very thing that was being depreciated by my denominational family—namely, the sacred Mystery that had summoned me in the first place. You hear this voice in these Heschel quotations:

> Our goal should be to live life in radical amazement...[to] get
> up in the morning and look at the world in a way that takes
> nothing for granted. Everything is phenomenal; everything

is incredible; never treat life casually. To be spiritual is to be amazed.[4]

The surest way to suppress our ability to understand the meaning of God and the importance of worship is to take things for granted. Indifference to the sublime wonder of living is the root of sin. Wonder or radical amazement is the chief characteristic of the religious man's attitude toward history and nature.[5]

A personal story captures the heart of his witness. Heschel, from a long line of Hasidic rabbis, spent most of his years as a teacher and writer at Jewish Theological Seminary in New York. When he was coming toward the end of his life, his rabbi friend Samuel Dresner visited him. Dresner writes, "Heschel spoke slowly and with effort…. 'I did not ask for success; *I asked for wonder*. And You [Yahweh] gave it to me.'"[6] Religion, as Heschel often said, is what we do with that wonder.

This experience of gracious mystery coupled with *a learned curiosity* of its meaning fuels scientists, philosophers, and, yes, theologians and preachers. Only from a "not knowing" stance can we understand—that is, standing under the generative wonder beyond our control.

How does this reframing translate into ministry?

You have your own ways of recovering radical amazement. Here are a couple of mine: I can either *lean in* or *step back*.

Leaning in means zooming in with curious questions, feeling the mystery of what is, anticipating with wonder what can be. If you wonder deeply enough, you will begin to awaken to gratitude, to insight, to amazement. In *preaching* you publicly wonder out loud. With curiosity you lean into the connection between the storied, biblical text and the storied life of congregants, expecting the birth of the new to happen. In *prophetic witness* you wonder in the face of evil, attempting to expose the falling short of shalom with a humility that confesses your limits of seeing and your need to learn from those who see differently. In *pastoral care* you lean in with wonder at a life being lived, offering attentive inquisitiveness, probing with the parishioner what new territory their crisis may be opening up to them. In *committee meetings* you lean in from a not-knowing position, equipped with sensitive questions that invite confidence and creativity. In *ordinary conversations* you lean in with open-heartedness, experiencing the wonder of what might awaken in these vulnerable exchanges.

Or you can *step back* and allow the radical amazement of any situation to sink in. Have you ever stepped back from glancing through the church directory or from scanning the congregation on a Sunday morning and felt the wonder of all these people choosing to volunteer their time, money, and love for a common cause? Have you ever paused in the pulpit with the Bible in hand and pondered the miracle of this document of multiple millennia? Or how about the miracle of your worship space bequeathed to the present congregation by those not present? Have you ever walked away from a family, whether profoundly grieving or celebrating, asking yourself, "How can people love so deeply and be loved so profoundly? Where does such capacity come from?" All of it is wondrous mystery! All of it is a wager that the Sacred permeates and saturates and illuminates all that lives, for "eyes that can see and ears that can hear," (Proverbs 20:12; Matthew 13:16) for those who will wonder deeply.

You can choose these stances at any time: the leaning in or the stepping back. With just a quick shift of awareness, you and I can feel the breathtaking gift of what or who is before you. Within a second you can go to that place of wonder, to radical amazement, to the mystery too deep for words. For such moments I've become fond of the phrase "This wonders me!" It's a simple practice for any moment of the day: to stand before any thing, any scene, any person, any glimpse in the mirror, any group, any place and allow it to "wonder you."

You and I are in the mystery business. It is not a measurable enterprise (as we experience at each annual evaluation of our ministry). With no small amount of courage, we marvel openly over this gracious mystery we name abundant life, love, forgiveness, God, Christ, Spirit, shalom, and we affirm this reality as the matrix "in which we live and move and have our being" (Acts 17:28). This is our calling: to work with unseen realities that cannot be captured in right believing. Jesus, our best embodiment of the love-justice of God, is the wondrous Mystery about which we keep telling stories. That's what we do; we keep telling stories.

I want this wager to set the tone for the remaining letters. For me, the shift from certainty to mystery, from willful knowing to learned curiosity, from correct believing to radical amazement, from attempts at controlling life to wagering one's life in surrender to Spirit as Love—this shift became a reframing, a prayer, for all the ministry that followed.

Nancy, our collegial friendship is rooted in the radical amazement we wager at the heart of our vocation. We share a calling that "wonders us."

With gratitude,
Mahan

Notes

[1] Rudolf Otto, *The Idea of the Holy* (book produced in EPUB format by the Internet Archive, 1996), 63.

Rudolf Otto's classic, first translated into English in 1923, is an inquiry into the non-rational experience of the divine holy, what he terms the "numinous" and captured in the phrase "mysterium tremendum et fascinans."

[2] William Shakespeare, Macbeth, (1605–1606)

[3] This is a Zen proverb, a teaching that words are like fingers pointing at the moon. If students look too closely at the fingers they never see the moon.

[4] Abraham Heschel, *God in Search of Man* (New York: Farrar, Straus & Cudahy, 1976), 46–47.

[5] Ibid., 43.

[6] Samuel Dresner, ed. *I Asked for Wonder: A Spiritual Anthology, Abraham Heschel* (New York: Crossroad, 1999), vii.

Section II

Living a Paradox:
Human and Symbolic Exemplar

Dear Nancy,

In this second section let's start at the beginning, the genesis of my venture into our vocation. I didn't know what I was getting into. You did. You grew up in a small, rural congregation that allowed close relationships with your pastors. Because of my lack of close-up experience, I thought being a pastor was similar to being a teacher or social worker. These roles of service make possible ways to contribute. So does being a pastor. That's the way I saw it.

I went to seminary with the joy of a new purpose to explore. I was given something larger to investigate and possibly love. I knew no one at the seminary when I arrived. Clergy were distant figures. Being Baptist was not significant. My church experience was more spectator than participant. The concept of "being called" was bewildering. But the idea of paid work for pursuing my two excitements—the Jesus vision of life and being with people in search of meaning—I found compelling.

My specific call to be a pastor of a congregation was sudden, spontaneous, very Baptist, and a bit bizarre. It is 1957. I am midway through my first year at Southern Baptist Theological Seminary. A letter from a lay leader at Coffee Creek Baptist Church in Paris Crossing, Indiana, is delivered to Dr. Wayne Oates (later to be my major professor during doctoral studies). The letter is a request for a seminary student, specifically a "single" student, to preach the following Sunday.

Being at the right place at the right time, I volunteer to fill the request. The next Sunday's drive is an easy fifty miles or so from Louisville. The day at Coffee Creek Baptist Church marks my first venture in leading services of worship, in this case both morning and evening. The day includes being initiated into the ritual of "preacher for lunch" with a host family that always includes the delight of home-fried chicken, roast beef, six or seven fresh vegetables, and a couple pies.

When I finish my responsibilities that evening and after a few minutes of small talk, I head for the car only to be intercepted by Charlie. "Preacher, hold on a minute, would you?" I comply with no clue as to what's happening. After about thirty minutes or so Charlie reappears. "A few of us deacons just had a quick meeting. We want to call you to be our pastor. We'll pay you fifty dollars a Sunday and eliminate the annual call." I have no idea what the annual call is, but it sounds like a huge fringe benefit. I dare not show my ignorance with a question. After all, they have just asked me to be their pastor. I'm thinking, why not? I'll see if this vocation fits. So "yes" it was.

During my return to Louisville that night, I kept whispering out loud, "I'm a pastor; I'm a pastor." All this change in one day. In one day my life turned.

In case you're curious about the specific request for a single man: Over time I discovered that the church receives more work from a single man than a married one; he is easier to entertain; and two very eligible and available young women were active in the congregation (Nancy, you always liked that part of the story).

Ordination in my home church soon followed. My ordination, with its language of "being set apart" to serve the church, declared more about my future than I could absorb at the time. I was unprepared for the projections that followed. Immediately, this new identity changed perceptions of me, particularly in Paris Crossing, the church community. Even my neighbors, family, and a few friends began to see me differently. Overnight, I was placed into a separate category that I didn't understand but most definitely felt.

At first I protested. I made every effort to minimize the "difference," the "set-apartness" that comes with the role of pastor. None of the titles felt comfortable—Brother Mahan, Preacher, Reverend, Pastor Siler. "Just call me Mahan," I kept saying. Occasionally I added something like, "I'm not different from you. I'm just a regular guy with a huge curiosity about life and faith." Over time, I gave that up. I came to tolerate the titles along with the minor and major projections that came with them.

A reframing appeared that made sense of these projections. Curiously, it came as a gift from a rabbi friend. The gift, a book written by another rabbi, Jack Bloom, gave me my first clear understanding of our role. In *Rabbi as Symbolic Exemplar* he names precisely the tension we carry. Rabbis (or pastors) are *living symbols of More than we are* and very ordinary *human beings*. We are both at the same time.[1]

A symbol points beyond itself to some other reality from which it draws power. Take our national flag, for instance. We know it's not simply a colorful piece of cloth. It draws our attention with the power of devotion to the "republic for which it stands." Or, even more familiar to us in the church, we regularly participate in the symbolic power of water (baptism) and bread and wine/grape juice (Eucharist).

Our symbolic power as pastors is public, for all to experience. Notice the scene: rabbis, priests, or pastors mounting the steps to a *pulpit* beneath a *robe* and *stole* (or dark suit) with *Scripture* in hand. There it is—the symbols, being a symbol of the Mystery. Yes, we are still very human under the robe and behind the pulpit with all our peculiar human traits in play. The sweat beneath the robe says as much. But we are so much more. We feel it. We know it. We are symbols of More Than We Are, signs of a narrative and worldview we call gospel. Or to say it boldly: You and I are symbols pointing to God, the ultimate Mystery. Simply by being and speaking as a clergy person, we declare a huge wager. We are asking others to wager with us that God is real, a loving presence in us, with us, between us, and through us, active in the world making love, making justice, and making shalom. We are symbols of that radical possibility.

Furthermore, our symbolic identity deepens with each passing funeral, wedding, worship service, and pastoral visit. We are walking, talking representatives of More Than Ourselves. And as you and I have noted, this symbolic role opens doors, and it also closes doors. It opens opportunities; it closes opportunities. We are set apart as different. Not better, but different. Not more important, but different. Not special human beings, but different.

And if that is not enough to carry, as pastors we are not just symbols; we are symbolic *exemplars*. We are to embody the Symbol. Certain ethical behaviors are expected of us. As the ordination of Episcopal clergy words it openly, we vow to be "wholesome examples" of the gospel. Leaders in other fields are also symbols of more than they are, but few leaders carry such additional moral expectation. Pastors, and in some sense their families, are expected to show, as well as tell, what loving God and neighbor looks like. We are expected to "walk the talk."

A further word about the family. The moral expectations fall upon the spouses and children as well. We have a title for the children—PKs, preachers' kids. They too, without their choosing, are "set apart." More, our families are in competition with the church for the time and emotional investment that pastoral work requires. On the positive side, friendship, instruction, and support can readily come from the congregation for the entire family. But let's name the flip side of the coin: the family comes under the aura of symbolic exemplar. Our vocation can be, and often is, a burden to our family. Because of the emotional demands of our work, I found this to be my greatest challenge: being fully present to my wife and four children.

Bloom puts the two together: the pastor or rabbi as *symbol* and as *exemplar*. Then he mixes in the third reality: We are symbolic exemplars and ordinary *human beings.* Underneath that robe, collar, and title is a personality with a unique set of peculiarities, abilities, and foibles. You and I are flawed symbols of More Than We Are. And these flaws, along with our gifts, are easy to see. Everyone in your congregation knows both your abilities and your faults. It comes with being a very, very public person.

Let's place Bloom's understanding on a continuum—symbolic exemplar on one end and human being on the other end. The extremes are easy to see.

On the symbolic exemplar end, we have observed pastors and priests overly identified with their symbolic role, so that much of their humanity is hidden behind their role. Their sense of self is fused, it seems, with their pastoral identity. "He must sleep in his collar," I recall it said of a Lutheran pastor in my neighborhood. At retirement, these ministers have the toughest work of finding themselves apart from the role. I admit that when I retired, this inner work of differentiation from this symbolic role was mine as well. I had to ask in a new way, "Who am I now?"

As you have, I found that there are times when this numinous power is undeniable. You know it when, on occasion, the message comes more through you than from you. Or when standing by the bed of a very ill parishioner or sitting across from a person in crisis, you palpably experience being a symbol of More Than Yourself. For them you represent their congregation and friends, not visible to them but present through you. You put a face to the Mystery of grace and the call to just relationships. When they see you, they "see" the unseeable realities you represent. In these times it's so clear that the parishioner is relating to you but also to so much More Than You.

Nancy, during my first years as pastor, I was wary about this authority. Who was I to speak for God? Who was I to assume this representative role? In addition, the abuses of this power in pastoral authority, so rampant among male clergy, tilted me in the other direction. God forbid I do that! More deeply, I feared losing myself in the role. In those early years I feared the seduction of being set apart as special, so I downplayed the appropriate authority asked of me. I never experienced this hesitation in you. This inner work was not yours to do.

Over time, I grew to value those moments that called for the full authority of the role. I am thinking of those occasions when we pastors are face-to-face with persons, usually in the safety of our offices, who pour out their sense of "not worthy," who are feeling particularly victim to self-condemning voices rising from their depths. Whenever I was experiencing their self-defeating voices, voices that to some degree are within us all, I knew I needed to draw from the highest authority possible. In those moments with a person feeling up against strong, oppressive, dominating self-destructive voices, I understood what the apostle Paul called "principalities and powers." In those moments, you and I have both found the pastoral authority that is precisely what's called for. We intentionally put on the "whole armor of God," (Ephesians 6:11) declaring for ourselves and for the one in our care a version of this affirmation: "What you tell yourself is not true. You are giving power to a lie. Your deepest truth is this: You are a child of God, loved and loving, forgiven and full of worth just as you are." By claiming fully this authority of God's compassion, I hear us praying that the Power that we name and symbolize will undermine and eventually replace the power of these life-denying, self-condemning voices. Part of our role encompasses the power to re-present the blessing of God's presence for healing, comfort, and transformation. However, I never spoke from such authority without "fear and trembling." The audacity is palpable.

Along with the angst of assuming this authority within our authorizing role, there's relief as well. This power is so clearly not about us. This healing energy is not ours to generate.

Less dramatically and more frequently, we assume this symbolic authority every time you and I rise to stand behind the pulpit and lead worship. We intentionally wrap around ourselves the privilege and courage of symbolizing the More Than Ourselves. We feel the difference. We are the messengers, not the message. We point. That's what we do: We point.

The other extreme of the continuum is highlighting our humanness. This is less complicated to describe. Simply put, to live from this end of the continuum is to discount the authority invested in the role. These pastors do all they can to downplay any difference, just as I did to begin with. "I'm just a person serving the church as a therapist or social worker serves a client. No difference except context."

Henri Nouwen's useful phrase, ministers as "wounded healers," has mistakenly inspired some pastors to lead with their wounds.[2] It's one thing to be vulnerable. It's another thing to give excessive attention to our wounds, especially in public. To deny the "set apart" difference and insist on being just a person like everyone else is folly. It's impossible. It's confusing to congregants. Furthermore, we forfeit opportunities that our role grants us.

In writing this letter I'm struck anew by the boldness of accepting this role. The mystics warn us that coming close to the Fire can burn as well as illumine. But we dare to come close. We dare to risk hubris in the hope of being relatively free of hubris in service to the other. We live within the challenge and tension of this both-and paradox of being both fully human and being a symbol and moral example.

Nancy, you and I are not in a collar-wearing tradition, but wearing the collar is a useful metaphor for us all. This I have observed from Episcopal and Roman Catholic priests: They wear the collar when taking on this symbolic role and don't wear the collar when they wish to minimize the difference. It illustrates the way of living this paradox: symbolic exemplar and human being.

To live this paradox demands chutzpah rooted in merciful grace; and merciful grace making possible the risk of chutzpah.

As those who dare to name the unnameable Mystery…
who embrace the tension of being a symbol of More yet fully human…
a flawed leader of an imperfect institution that frequently
contradicts the compassion it declares…
and bearing the symbols of God, even being a
symbol of God at the perilous risk of playing
God…
Lord, have mercy. Christ, have mercy.

With gratitude,
Mahan

Notes

[1] Jack H. Bloom, *The Rabbi as Symbolic Exemplar* (Binghamton, NY: The Haworth Press, 2003).
This Letter to Nancy, with translation, reflects precisely Rabbi Bloom's message to other rabbis.

[2] Nouwen, J.M, *The Wounded Healer* (New York, NY: Doubleday, 1979).
Henri Nouwen challenges healers, like pastors, to acknowledge and work with the healing of their own wounds. From that humility and self-awareness healers can connect with the wounded others. I caution against the temptation to display the wounds. It's a delicate balance: leading with vulnerability without undue attention to our wounds.

Pastor to Pastoral Leader

Dear Nancy,

This letter, perhaps more than others, reflects the generational difference between the two of us. My transition from pastor to pastoral leader seems to be more in place in your generation and the current generation of pastors. When I was a seminary, there was no course offered in leadership. Today, the assumption of leadership is better incorporated in theological education and well may be a clearer expectation by laity as well.

If you had known me as a beginning pastor and had asked me if I were a leader, my response would have been immediate: "Of course I am. It comes with the call from a congregation to be its pastor."

Actually, it was only midway through my vocation that I made a conscious decision to claim my identity as pastoral leader. "Being a pastor" was my first and most compelling identity. The memory of when that self-identity fell into place is vivid. The setting is an introductory course in pastoral care in the large map room, Norton Hall, at Southern Baptist Theological Seminary in 1957. The professor, Wayne E. Oates, is unpacking a typical pastoral situation in front of a class of about thirty students. As I recall, the person receiving his care was distraught over the abrupt death of her husband. I remember leaning forward, intrigued and curious, saying under my breath, "I want to do that!" And I have, in some form, for sixty years.

The title *pastor* resonated then and still does now over sixty years later. For me this identity has a vibrancy and energy I don't feel from other titles assigned to me. In early days it was "Rev," "Brother Mahan," or just "Preacher." Later, "Senior Minister," with its feel of aloofness, never took hold. Neither does "Doctor," with its confusion: "What kind of doctor are you?"

My seminary experience gave me plenty of *functional* identities to study: preacher, teacher, prophet, pastor, manager, counselor, liturgist, and community leader. During my first years I juggled these roles, valuing each one, attempting them all, but feeling fragmented most of the time. At that time I thought of leadership as managing the institutional side of church. For me it was the rent I had to pay for the joy of preaching, teaching, leading worship, offering pastoral care, and contributing some leadership in the community.

This I discovered: Simply being a pastor is an insufficient pole around which to wrap these many functions. It didn't work for me. "Pastor" was not an integrating core identity. The fragmentation led to over-functioning, and over-functioning led to emotional and spiritual exhaustion.

For ten years I was in between my seasons as pastor. As you know, during most of that decade, I was director of a department within a medical system that included both hospital and medical school. My role was clear: I was a leader of a subsystem, a department of the hospital. My position as director was clear. The boundaries were clear. The expectations were clear. I was paid to lead. During that period I studied leadership. I had to. It was the role required of me. By the time I returned to congregational life as pastor at Pullen, I had changed. I finally saw myself as a pastoral leader. You experienced me as a pastoral leader. It was a reframing that mattered profoundly.

The pastor as leader holds a particular place in the body of the congregation. The apostle Paul's systematic view of the church is helpful here. He wrote of the church as a body having many parts, such as hands and arms and legs. Each part contributes to and depends on all the other functions of the body. To build on Paul's organic understanding of the church, the role of pastoral leader holds a distinct position in the body—namely, the eyes. I find it informative that one of the early titles for pastoral leader is *bishop*, meaning "overseer." We can see why. Because of your function in the congregational system, you are able to "see over" the body of the congregation like no one else. Other members can see from their particular angle, but no one has the overview like the pastoral leader does. We are set apart with time, gifts, and education to see the whole picture, both of the congregation and of its place in the world.

Ronald Heifetz and Marty Linsky, writers and students of leadership, offered me a similar image. Leaders regularly must leave the "dance floor" where the congregations is interacting as if dancing in pairs, small groups, and larger circular dances. Leaders, he insists, must get to the balcony where they can oversee the dance floor.[1] This, in part, is what we are paid to do. As you and I have noted, to give this time and value is hard to do. We both love being active on the dance floor. It feels like taking us away from ministry to leave the important interactions on the dance floor and find time to reflect on the life of the whole congregation. Yet it is only from the balcony that we can see the big picture. Only from the balcony can we observe patterns, both what's lifegiving and what's not. Only from the balcony can we see the interplay between the congregation and the local community.

By the time we began working together in 1992, I had internalized this reframe. My primary identity was *pastoral leader partnering with other staff and lay leaders*. It provided the pole around which I could wrap the various functions of ministry. I felt integrated in ways I had not in earlier years.

As *preacher* and *liturgist*, along with others you led weekly by addressing not only individual members and families but also the congregational system. Each service of worship is an intervention of leadership in life together. Think about it, Nancy. What executive leaders in corporate organizations have the weekly opportunity to address their systems directly in person? We do. Regularly, we are allowed to engage the congregation in ways of being church. To some degree each individual member leaves corporate worship changed. Yes, that's hopefully true. But so does the congregation. In leading worship, you are leading the congregation.

In *pastoral care*, I imagine you leading with the awareness that change in one life affects change in all the relational networks or systems in which that person lives—family, friends, congregation, work, neighbors, community, nation, globe. If that person or marriage or family moves toward maturation, so does the congregation. Your pastoral care impacts the life of the congregation. So does the lack of effective pastoral care.

As *prophetic pastor*, I see you engaging the battle over worldviews. You offer an alternative way to see the world in the face of these strong competitive world-views: fundamentalism, with its certainty; salvation through technology; safety through military dominance; security through material possessions; globalism through corporate capitalism. You message a counter worldview. You attend to the interior life that will externalize in the world as compassion, mercy, and justice.

Yes, of course, you invite individual persons to this worldview. But more to the point, you help lead a congregation to embody this vision as closely as possible. You invite the church to show what a community of God's mercy and justice looks like. You call the congregation to be not a collection of individual disciples but the body of Christ.

As *manager*, with others you lead not only with the question of doing the right things but also with the managerial question of doing the right things well. A smooth-working congregation is critical. But you lead with a likely difference. While others are prone to see individuals or families or subgroups as separate, you see relationships. When you are sitting in a committee meeting, seeing with the eyes of an overseer, you will be computing how an action is likely to play out throughout the entire church body. You may be the only one in the room who knows that change at one point affects change at all points. In a committee meeting, for instance, you participate in making decisions with the larger congregation in mind. You may be the one to ask, "How does this management decision align with our mission statement, our reason for being?"

As *community leader*, you study how your congregation interfaces with the various organizations within the community. You show up as representative of your congregation, looking for ways to connect and partner with community efforts that share common values and visions.

In each of these functions you are leading. In each function you are affecting the relational system of the congregation. Only the forms and contexts of leadership vary.

When I began my time at Pullen, I received a helpful piece of advice from a professor schooled in leadership. Bob Dale said, "Mahan, your challenge will be how to lead from the past." Indeed, in the almost hundred years of our congregation, there was much to name and bring forward for wisdom and motivation. He was challenging me not to see leadership only as future-oriented. That would overlook the resourceful past. I began to look back in our history for what leaders, what decisions, what processes for decision-making, what failures, what breakthroughs happened that could be accessed for current challenges.

As the current pastoral leader of this same congregation, you know well the wisdom of leading from the past. But it's your choice as leader to decide what parts of the past to access. Bob's advice was not to live the past but to lead *from* the past, to draw from history in ways that fortify and inspire the present congregation facing its future. And do it intentionally.

All these functions of leading are about doing. I hasten to add the importance of *presence*—being present, including at times as a playful presence. Let's not underestimate the power of showing up, here and there, with the capacity to be a presence relatively free of anxiety and reactivity. We have considered in the prior reframe that our presence always has a measure of the More Than We Are. That's incorporated into our sense of presence. The attentiveness, confidence, curiosity, and hope experienced in one's presence just may be the most underrated gift of leadership.

Integration has been the subject of this reframe. When I made this shift in self-identity from pastor to pastoral leader, I felt integrated for the first time. I came to appreciate that all the varied functions of ministry were ways to leading a congregation and its mission in the world. I was a pastoral leader. You are a pastoral leader.

With gratitude,
Mahan

Note

[1] Ronald A. Heifetz and Marty Linsky, *Leadership on the Line* (Boston, MA: Harvard Business Review Press, 2002), 51–74.

Heifetz and Linsky give a chapter to this metaphor—"getting off the dance floor and going to the balcony." It's the capacity, often in the midst of action, to ask, "What's really going on here?" This skill to distance yourself from the fray, taking yourself from the dance for a balcony perspective is a capacity to practice. The challenge is to move back and forth between the dance floor and balcony, being as close as you can be in both places simultaneously.

Agents of Change

Dear Nancy,

You know this about my history: In my first attempt in pastoral ministry I "burned out." I overfunctioned to the point that I felt up against the choice between church and family responsibilities. I chose family. But in my last season of ministry, shared with you for almost half of the fifteen years, I ended vital and grateful. A major difference, I suggest, is understanding systems thinking that I received from Edwin Friedman and his mentor, Murray Bowen.

Change is at the core of our vocation. We hear it in weighty words like *repentance, conversion, redemption, transformation,* and *reconciliation.* But how change occurs is complex, more mystery than not. I came out of seminary excited, feeling ready to be an agent of change. The search committee that offered me my first full-time pastoral opportunity shared a similar expectation. They proposed, "Here is where we are as a congregation. Here is where we want to be." The subliminal message I heard was, "Your leadership can change us and help us change the world." So I set about to be an agent of *their* change so we could change the world.

But along the way—about four years in—I began to question my capacity to change "the other." It didn't work. A particular change might be willed for a period, but when the pressure was released, the behavior went back to previous patterns. It didn't work for my wife, not for my children, not for friends, not for the congregation, and not for myself. Any willful effort to change always invited the counterforce of resistance. Clearly, something was missing in my view of change.

What was missing—and it became a reframing that mattered—is understanding change from a systems perspective. It speaks a counterintuitive message: Focus on yourself, not your congregation, which, as strange as it seems, invites change in the congregation. You work on yourself—your clarity of vision, your learning, your integrity, your transformation, your responses, your relationships, your questions, your calling, your presence. It all sounds totally self-serving and selfish until you see the paradox: By working on changing yourself within relationships, you change the system. By focusing on our functioning in relationships, we change the relationships. This perspective—centering on changing self, not congregation—felt like a 180-degree turn. It was.

Let's review the systems view of change. Imagine a system as a mobile with various hanging, dangling parts. We know from experience that if the height of one part is changed, then the entire mobile is changed. All the parts of the mobile are thrown out of balance until the force of togetherness (homeostasis) brings the parts into balance again, but all of them in slightly new positions.

Remember a sermon in which you took a stand that challenged the congregation. It was a new position you were taking, like changing your part of the mobile. The sermon was unsettling. The congregation, like a mobile, was thrown out of balance, however slightly. But you also noticed, either immediately or over time, that there was a power in the congregational system at work, pulling toward a new stability. The mobile-like congregation eventually settles down into a new balance, somewhat changed.

Or consider this metaphor: Imagine a number of separate parts connected to each other by rubber bands. Let's say that one part proceeds upward to a new position with the other parts feeling also pulled in the that direction. Notice what happens. All the rubber bands, not just one, feel the stretch or challenge. One of three reactions will occur: One option is that all the other parts resist, and with their collective strength they pull the deviant part back to the familiar level of what had been. A second option is that the deviant part stretches so far that a few of the connecting rubber bands break, called by systems theorists a "cut off," a disconnection. The stretch or change was too radical for the rest of the rubber bands to tolerate. A third possibility is that the pull of the adventurous part will provoke a change among the other parts in its direction.

Think again of that same visionary sermon you preached. Notice the options: Did your vision get no traction, no movement of change from the system, with congregants saying in effect, "We are not ready for that"? The congregation pulled you back and you were left saying, "I'll wait for another time." Or was the vision so "far out" that it was rejected, "cut off" like the break of a rubber band? Or was there enough curiosity and excitement from congregants for there to be significant movement toward the vision articulated in the sermon?

Each metaphor illustrates the central point: Changing yourself, your position in any relational system, changes in some way the relational system as a whole, whether it's two people or an entire congregation.

While we cannot change the other, we can offer with clarity the changes occurring in us in a way that invites the possibility of significant change happening in them. We challenge the other by *defining our self in relationships*.

Note this difference: To try to change another is to say, "This is what I think you should believe or do or be." It's a "you" message. To focus on our self is to send an "I" message. The message "Here is where I am with (issue, situation, belief, conflict). This is what I see or feel" contains an inherent invitation: "Where are *you* with this? What do *you* see or feel?" By focusing on defining yourself and offering that self-awareness, you challenge the other person or persons to do the same—namely, to take responsibility for defining themselves. Again, the paradox: When you are free from trying to change the other, you grant the other the freedom to change.

This is the essential interaction: "This is what I see; what do you see?" It's present in preaching: "This is what I see in this text; what do you see?" Or in a committee meeting: "This is where I see the connection with our mission; how about you?" These interactions strengthen *mutual* capacity to take responsibility for our thinking, feeling, and doing.

But this is an important clarity. This focus on self is *not* to be confused with autonomy or independence or self-differentiation alone. In systems thinking, according to Murray Bowen and his interpreter Ed Friedman, a self is a *connected self*, a self in relationship. *The self is always in relationship*, like the parts of a mobile and the rubber bands of my two metaphors. There is no such thing as a separate self. I once heard Friedman muse, "Maybe life is all about *how to be a self in relationship*."[1] That's the heart of it. That's the challenge of it. It's the essence of leadership.

Being a self in relationship captures the paradox. You are both connected—that is, in relationship—and you are a differentiated self—that is, a separate self in the relationship. The dangers are obvious: You can lose yourself in overfocusing on the relationship, or you can lose the relationship by overfocusing on self-differentiation.

I found in this reframe both a *gift* and *cost*. The gift is the energy you save in not working to change the other. It's a simpler, less anxious way to lead a congregation. Willful leadership is exhausting. There is relief in realizing that we cannot motivate people to change, as if we know what others need to become. It's freeing, not wearying, to stay focused on questioning, challenging, offering, and inviting.

A second gift is understanding societal changes, not just congregational. The systemic understanding of change reminds us how slow, erratic, and messy social change actually is. Every movement toward justice—racial and gender equity, as an example—creates a counterforce to uphold the status quo. Those who experience change as loss of comfort, privilege, and shared core beliefs will dig in and resist. A systems view of change helps us work with the resistance and take the long view, sometimes a very long confidence in the "arc that bends toward justice." King's faith in an arc that bends, not breaks, fits a systems view of change.

While the gift of this reframe is huge, I experienced *cost* from it as well. I did so in four ways:

1. You will inevitably "see" differently than others do; conflict is inevitable. And if the differences become heated, then your work is how to stay connected without requiring agreement. It is costly, hard work to stay in relationship when differences are being mutually voiced and felt. Expect conflict. Expect to be changed. Even come to appreciate it as the way significant, systemic change actually happens. It requires time, patience, vulnerability, and detachment from outcome.

2. When you challenge from a place of "this is what I see," expect resistance. Friedman notes that when clarity of a position occurs, the next thing to look for are efforts to sabotage.[2] After all, you are inviting discomfort in the service of maturity. This goes against our human tendency to reduce conflict rather than encourage difference. Some congregants, and perhaps staff colleagues as well, prefer the comfort of the familiar to the dis-ease of change. I'm told that when there are many crabs in a net and one moves toward the opening and thus freedom, the other crabs will pull it back. For sure, this is a dynamic in human systems. Expect serious work with resistance when you attempt leadership through self-differentiation.

3. Don't underestimate the time, maturity, and effort it takes to find the space within yourself to clarify your vision and your responses to others' reactions. This work of self-definition is demanding. It's spiritual work. To react from our oldest "reptilian" part of the brain is quick and easy; to respond with thought-through, non-anxious words and presence reflects years of inner work.

4. Challenging others with what you see, along with the invitation for them to do the same while staying in relationship—well, that's a

tall order. It's an unrealistic ideal to expect such maturity from everybody, including yourself, all the time. Leading from self-differentiation will elicit multiple responses from those around you: Some people will be unable to respond with "I" statements; others will experience your self-definition as coercive; some will misinterpret your intent and content; some will blame you for challenging the status quo. The stretch of the "rubber band" may be too much, too fast, too threatening. No one told me this expression of intentional leadership could reap so much misunderstanding and, at times, loneliness.

While systems thinking altered my understanding of change, I had to look elsewhere to find the inner strength required to adopt it. To approximate leading from a place of both clarity and non-anxiousness requires spiritual practices that anchor us in an inner identity as beloved, an identity not attached to results. I turned to contemplative prayer. I'll write to you about this resource in a latter letter.

This letter has been largely theoretical. I insist that this theory is immensely practical. So I close with an example, perhaps my clearest effort to apply this view of leadership in a critical situation.

Nancy, you know this story and its consequences. You joined the ministerial staff a few months after the congregation decided to add the ritual of blessing of a gay union, what we would call now a gay marriage. This is not a success story. Systems theory is not about success or failure. It's about how change happens.

In 1986 I preached a sermon from the text of the parable of the good Samaritan, proposing that homosexuals were the good Sanitarians of our day who had the position of potentially healing us from our homophobic oppression of gays. In a welcoming relationship with them, I suggested, we can be healed. That sermon opened a door through which I walked into unexpected public advocacy for gay and lesbian equality. Now it would include bisexual and transgender persons. Because of this turn in my ministry, I knew eventually there would be a couple asking for a union (marriage) ceremony.

A gay couple made such a request in fall 1991. I intentionally followed a systems understanding of leadership. Kevin, Stephen, and I spent a month probing their readiness, both for a marriage commitment and for the possibility of being a focus of controversy. We were working on self-definition. Once I concluded that their request for a public ceremony of worship with family and friends was not motivated by something different to opposite-sex couples who wish to marry, I next worked on my self-definition. For at least a month I searched for my own clarity. As pastor, what was I called to do? My motivation? This timing? I looked at all the angles. I decided to move forward.

Next, following Baptist congregational polity, I took their request to the deacons (lay leadership), saying the request for this ritual was their decision to make. I pledged my support of their process. I also made available to them my self-definition—namely, the reasons why I thought the ritual of covenant love was a place for our church to take a stand. From that point on, I did not speak publicly in favor of the request. For those interested, my opinion was written and available. This freed me to attend to their process of discernment.

After six weeks of confidential deliberation, the deacons, by a vote of fourteen to five—another layer of self-definition—took their recommendation to the congregation along with a process for the church's own self-definition. This took about three months of discernment. Not intentionally, the congregation's self-definition and eventual decision became a catalyst that challenged other congregations and Christians far and wide to self-define. From more than 300 messages we received, a few were affirming. Most were opposed, if not condemning.

From all appearances this process felt and looked stressful and chaotic largely because of the media coverage and Southern Baptist outrage. But for eyes that could see, there was a clear red thread that ran throughout the process. At each stage, there was self-definition within relationships where enough persons were risking "This is what I see, believe, and feel; what do you see, believe, and feel?" Here's the painful, heartbreaking part: Some members—about a sixth of the congregation—defined themselves out of Pullen.

All the promises and costs from this systems theory process listed above were at play. But if I had tried to change the congregation to what I believed, then the difficult discernment process would have been about me. It would have been reduced to the issue of gay marriage, not to how will we be in relationship with both the gay couple and each other in this process. It's a story of change from within congregational relationships. It's a story of self-differentiation while staying connected. It's a story of much cost and much promise.

This, I add in closing, may be my most important word: Treat systems thinking like a language. Because each aspect is counterintuitive, it takes time to internalize this theory. While in current theological education this view of leadership is always included, it unlikely sticks to the bone. To learn systems thinking is no easier than learning a foreign language. It takes practice, preferably with other pastoral leaders.

Nancy, this is a lot to include in one letter. For you, it's just a review of many conversations we have had about this theory. For others sufficiently interested, there is an ample supply of clear interpreters of systems theory for leaders of congregation. I recommend, in addition to Friedman, Peter Steinke, Israel Galindo, Ron Richardson, and Gilbert Rendle.

You well know from working with me that this systems theory, like a pair of glasses, changed the way I saw leadership. You will find aspects of it showing up in subsequent letters. But in addition, this counterintuitive wisdom reframed my understanding of the changes occurring in all relationships.

With gratitude,
Mahan

Notes

[1] I heard this comment from Edwin H. Friedman—"Maybe life is all about how to be a self in relationship"—in a lecture on pastoral leadership at Wake Forest University in May, 1990. These words seemed an unintended side comment.

[2] Edwin H. Friedman, *Failure of Nerve: Leadership in the Age of the Quick Fix* (New York: Seabury Books, 2007), 11, 19, 94, 189, 191.

While working on his last manuscript Friedman gave lectures on his view of leadership as self-differentiation while remaining in relationships from a non-anxious presence. I attended some of these lectures in the early 1990s and listened to the tapes religiously. Working with the resistance or sabotage, often the first reaction to self-defined leadership, is a key theme in Friedman. He died on October 31, 1996 before he could complete this manuscript. However, a few of his students worked with the unfinished manuscript to make this publication possible. This book is a summation of his latest ideas and needs to be read alongside his earlier groundbreaking application of family systems theory to clergy leadership, *Generation to Generation*, 1985.

The Congregation's Angel

Dear Nancy,

This letter comes at systems thinking from a surprising direction. But first let's set the stage.

You remember the hand gesture, locking your fingers inward and saying, "This is the church; this is the steeple," and then, as you open your hands, "open the door; here's all the people"?

I suspect that for most people the church appears as an aggregate of individuals. When you look out over the congregation on a Sunday morning, what do you see? You see individuals separated in rows, each with a distinct appearance, each with a different personality, and each with a different history. Looking through the church pictorial directory, you notice individual faces, most of whom are shown with family members, each with different names. In your imagination when your congregation comes to mind, you likely think of individuals to call or families to visit.

But on some level we know there's more. Intuitively, we know church to be more than separate individuals and family units. We just know it. There's an invisible reality that will never show up in a church directory or even in group pictures.

To make the point, imagine with me two fictitious individuals reflecting on their first visits to an unfamiliar congregation: One says, "I walked down the aisle, found a seat, looked around, breathed in the ambiance of the space, glanced through the worship bulletin, and took a deep breath. I don't know why, but I just felt at home. This fits. I could be a member here, I thought."

The other says, "The people seemed nice enough. The sermon was okay. Nothing wrong with the music. But, somehow, I didn't feel engaged. I'm not sure what I am looking for, but this is not the congregation for me."

This felt, invisible force that each of these church visitors experienced, we could call by a number of names: "culture," "spirit," "corporate personality," or the "gravitas" of a congregation. Walter Wink calls this reality the "angel" of a congregation.[1] Wink's interpretation of angel—new to me—immediately became a reframe that mattered.

Angel? Angel of a congregation? Who believes in angels these days? Aren't angels disembodied figments of a non-enlightened mind? What possible meaning could this ethereal construct have for us?

Walker Wink is convincing. He opened my eyes to an added dimension of congregational life. This New Testament scholar wrote a trilogy that shook the theological world, including my theological worldview: *Naming the Powers* (1984), *Unmasking the Powers* (1986), and *Engaging the Powers* (1992). In *Unmasking the Powers*, Wink notices that in chapters two and three of the book of Revelation, seven letters are sent to the seven churches in Asia Minor. But they are addressed to the "angel" of each congregation. In contrast, Paul addresses his letters to an entire congregation, like to the church at Ephesus or the church at Philippi. Until Wink's observation, I had never noticed this difference.

For Wink, the angel of each congregation represents its totality. The angel is not something separate or moralistic or airy. Rather, the congregation is the angel's incarnation. The angel of a church is embodied in flesh-and-blood people who occupy a particular place. The angel represents the spirituality of a congregation, its corporate personality, its interiority, its felt sense of the whole. *Angel* (angelos) in this context means "messenger." The angel of a church conveys its true unvarnished message. It tells it like it is, the good and not so good.[2]

In the above illustration of the fictitious visitors, these individuals encountered the angel of the same congregation. They engaged its spirit or culture. One visitor didn't connect with the angel. The other person did, experiencing a coming-home feeling.

The angel in each of the seven churches in Revelation reveals in these congregations a mixture of maturity and immaturity. In the letters to these congregations, Christ's spirit is addressing the angels of these congregations with both affirmation and challenge. For example, to the *angel of Ephesus*: "I know your works, your toil and your patient endurance...[but] you have abandoned the love you had at first" (Rev 2:2). To the *angel of Laodicea*, the message begins with a scathing indictment: "I wish you were either cold or hot. So because you are lukewarm, and neither cold nor hot, I am about to spit you out of my mouth. For you have said, I am rich, I have prospered, and I need nothing. You do not realize that you are wretched pitiable, poor, blind and naked." Ouch! That's a hard-hitting message. And then comes the encouragement: "I reprove and discipline those whom I love. Be earnest, therefore, and repent. Listen, I am standing at the door, knocking; if you hear my voice and open the door, I will come in to you and eat with you, and you with me" (Rev 3:16, 20).

Each letter ends with the same challenge: "Let everyone who has an ear, listen to what the Spirit is saying to the churches."

Although this reflection focuses on congregations, it is important to note that every collective entity has an angel. A family or a business has its own unique spirit, as does a school. We even speak of "school spirit." Wink gives us a way to name the invisible spirituality within any visible institution. Wink reclaims a biblical image—granted, an unfamiliar one—for naming this invisible reality as angel.

This is the picture: In all seven letters in the book of Revelation, Christ is imaged as walking among the congregations, engaging the angel of each, sometimes critically, sometimes affirmatively—all in the service of transforming the angel into Christlikeness. We are accustomed to focusing on the grace of Christ at work in the lives of individual persons. But also, as Wink reminds us, this Spirit is at work loving, confronting, healing, and transforming the spirit-angel of each congregation.

Now let's turn to the significance of this reframe for our leadership as pastor, for this awareness I received from Wink dovetails perfectly with family systems theory that I described in the previous reframe. As the new pastor of Pullen, my last congregation and your present congregation, I set before myself two tasks: *to come to know the people and to come to know the system*, the corporate spirit that I later learned from Wink to be the angel of the church.

The second task felt like detective work. I looked for clues of the angel. I noted the architecture, the placement of pulpit, choir, and other symbols. What's the message they tell about our spirit-angel? I kept asking questions: What's the glue that holds us together? I listened for favorite stories about past events, past crises, and past pastors. What former rituals continue to be life-giving? And what are people in the larger community saying about us?

A particular clarity soon surfaced from my exploration of our almost century of congregation life: Our angel had two strong wings—attention to worship and attention to social justice. This core awareness served as a reference point for the rest of my leadership.

This was my assumption: The angel, if I allowed it, was introducing itself to me. I was being invited less to analyze the angel than to learn to love the angel. In what may appear strange, I was forming a close relationship with the angel, as well as with the people. I was loving who we are together, not only those individuals who gathered. This curiosity had all the ingredients of courting another in the hope for a long relationship. I was given the privilege to love this particular congregation—with all its complexities, gifts, failures, inconsistencies, and richness. You share that privilege, Nancy.

Perhaps some specific examples will help you understand the value of this double vision—*seeing individual persons* and *seeing the invisible corporate spirit, the angel.*

I first experienced the angel of Pullen as cool, reluctant to extend a warm welcome to visitors. The church had been through some stressful years that had consumed the energy that otherwise would have been more available to newcomers. When the congregation gathered for worship, members wanted to be together, to support and enjoy each other. Wink gave me language for what I was intuiting—namely, a wound in our angel that needed healing. For the next decade, a priority for our leaders was to recover the church's former generosity and eagerness to welcome the stranger.

This angel was severely tested in my ninth year. I wrote about this in the previous letter. As I noted there, the congregation was discerning whether or not to add a ritual to our ministry—the blessing of a same-sex union. At the time, there was not a more contentious, divisive issue in the larger church. This was the surprise: During this extended process of decision-making, we experienced more conflict *outside* the congregation than *within* it.

I wondered then and now what kept us "steady in the water" during this whirlwind of controversy. I believe it was the angel of Pullen. During those stressful months, often a member would say something like, "Yes, we will lose some members. Yes, we will lose some money, just like we did when we elected women deacons in the 1940s and when we racially integrated in the late 1950s and when our pastor was speaking out against the Vietnam War in the late 1960s. We made it through then. We'll make it through now." The angel, with its passion for social justice, rooted in its favorite passages—Micah 6:8 and Jesus's mission statement in Luke 4—proved to be the steady, broad keel that kept our ship from overturning in turbulent waters. Enough members said, "We are being true to who we are by discerning our relationship with gay persons [LGBTQ]." They were referring to our angel.

This imaginative metaphor of a congregation's spirit inspired my occasional sermon that addressed the angel of our congregation. A couple years before you came, in a 1990 sermon drawing on Wink's interpretation of these verses in the book of Revelation, I imaged Christ walking among us, engaging our angel. I spoke of Christ's affirmation of our angel's heart for the community, a passion that arose from regularly worshiping a God active for justice and mercy. I offered some specific examples of this rhythm between worship and service.

But I also pictured Christ confronting our angel for its pride in feeling special, unique, progressive, and superior. Not to the pleasure of Christ do we take our importance so seriously. I also envisioned our angel being chastised for being, at times, so open and inclusive that such grace morphed into cheap grace with little cost, minimal sacrifice, and shallow commitment.

And I ended the sermon, "These are my reflections on our angel. What's more important is that you take away this image of the spirit of Christ encountering our collective spirit, walking among us with the desire to transform our angel into his likeness. It's a place to meet for further conversation among us."

I conclude this letter by noting a peculiar characteristic of our work, Nancy. Like few vocations, pastoral ministry is all about seeing the unseeable. The realities of trust, hope, and love—indeed, the Mystery we name God—are all invisible Spirit, like the wind, an uncontrollable force sought and experienced but not seen. Even the forces at work in interpersonal relationships, the very heart of our work, cannot be seen or precisely measured. In this letter I am underscoring yet another invisible reality on the list: the angel of each congregation.

I recommend the reframe: continuing to discern and love the angel, in your case Pullen congregation, in the service of further transformation as the body of Christ.

With gratitude,
Mahan

Notes

[1] Walter Wink, *Unmasking the Powers* (Minnenpolis: Fortress Press, 1986), 69–86.

[2] The tenor of these messages of Christ to the angel of each of the seven congregations is strikingly confrontational. In contrast the Apostle Paul in his letters to congregations is more personal, pastoral in his affirmations and challenges.

Hospice Chaplain/Midwife

Dear Nancy,

In a circle of pastors, I asked this question: "Your current ministry feels like a… *what*?" It's the kind of question you have often heard from me. Pete's response has stayed with me. He said, "I feel like a hospice chaplain and a midwife."

Since then, I've tested his metaphor. Now I am testing it with you. It may be a metaphor that fits more now than when I was in the pastoral role. As I listen to pastors, the metaphor consistently rings true. In my work with clergy during my retirement, it has become for me a reframe of the role. While no metaphor captures the complexity of our work, this reframe is worth exploring. Let's look at both images separately.

Hospice chaplains help people die. If possible, they seek to help people die within the awareness of being loved. They invite dying with grace and gratitude for their life lived. These specialists come alongside the dying and align with forces of medicine, faith, confession, forgiveness, and community. You know this sacred work with parishioners.

But Pete was not referencing this aspect of pastoral grief work. Pete was pointing to another level of loss that is particularly characteristic of our historical moment.

You hear this grief in these typical laments from church members:
- "We don't have young people like we used to."
- "I miss the old hymns."
- "You don't talk about God in ways I'm accustomed to hearing."
- "We are not comfortable with a woman's voice in the pulpit."
- "Even our 'active' members only attend maybe twice a month."
- "Why, we used to have a thriving Sunday school."
- "Nobody talks about tithing anymore."
- "People don't give of their time and money like they used to."
- "Change is everywhere. Does it have to be in the church too?"

Pete was astute with his metaphor. He saw in all the rapid changes the experience of loss. We know this about change: We resist change because we resist loss. Pete was picking up on feelings of loss among congregants: the loss of church status, once mainline, now sidelined; the loss of educational programs, once vital but now less so; the loss of confidence in institutions, especially among the younger generation; the loss of generous financial giving to the church, once assumed but now less so; and the loss of denominational allegiance, once important, now insignificant for most members.

There is a deeper, not so obvious loss. It's theological and perhaps unconscious. Persons in the pew are struggling with the basics of faith in a way that was not the case when I began pastoral ministry. In Pullen and in the congregations of pastors who read these letters, I post this assumption: These particular beliefs are being challenged—God as supernatural being up there, out there; humans as the center and point of creation; Christianity as the true religion; Christianity as singularly about individual salvation; the Bible as consistent, not contradictory; you can add to the list. Christians in our day are being pressed to reflect on cherished beliefs. Their foundations are shaking. Some seize the opportunity. Others dig in and resent the challenge of this inner, theological work.

Jesus references the "winnowing fan that separates the grain from the chaff" (Matt 3:12). Isn't this a part of what you do? You help parishioners separate the wheat from the chaff, letting go what's not alive and retaining what's lifegiving. Each letting go is a loss. Each one is an experience of dying. It's grief work. It's hospice chaplaincy. With patience and tender care you invite members to grieve the loss of what was but no longer contains vitality for them.

I'm guessing that you didn't "sign on" to be a hospice chaplain. I didn't either. With this ministry so obvious now, you may be considering the priority it deserves.

That brings us to the second half of Pete's metaphor: "I am a midwife." Pete, in explaining his metaphor, felt the excitement of a midwife (as much as a man can know this experience). He saw himself alongside "pushes" for birthing the new that, here and there, was happening within the congregation. There were ideas, events, and practices put forward as experiments. And within the larger church there are efforts, like the Emerging Church movement, to engage this hunger for new ways of being church in our day. For Pete this role of midwife meant the opportunity to assist parishioners in birthing the new—new programs, new structure, and new understandings of God, prayer, church, and discipleship.

If Pete's metaphor resonates with you, let's turn it around in our minds for a moment.

At first glance this metaphor—hospice chaplain and midwife—appears binary, as if it is either one or the other. Not so. It's not as if we do grief hospice work in the morning and midwifing of the new in the afternoon. It's not a stance toward the past and then shifting to a stance toward the future. Rather, the metaphor is a paradox, a both-and at the same time.

Our theology helps us at this point. The church has named this paradox the Paschal Mystery—the mystery of dying and rising, death and resurrection. In contrast to binary thinking, this tradition declares that life comes out of death over and over again. Life never dies. Love never dies. The forms die, but not the life and love within them.

Perhaps our stance of faith can help us hold together what on the surface feels to be a polarity. As both hospice chaplain and midwife, you embody the connection between the letting go in dying and the welcoming of new life. You experience it. You know this to be the way both faith and evolution work—dying and rising, death preceding life, life coming out of death. The womb must be painfully died to, left behind, for birth to occur. If held too long in the womb, there is no new life. There is only death. (This occasional reality requires that we hold this metaphor tenderly.)

Being both a hospice chaplain and a midwife is a precarious place to be. From standing in that breach as bridge-leader, you cannot expect much understanding or appreciation from either direction. We can see why. Who likes to hear the message that there's dying occurring in the church or, more to the point, that there is dying happening within them? Who is eager to hear the firm, gentle invitation to let go and trust the new that is yet to be formed? The denial of death, perhaps our favorite human defense, will flex its muscles. Expect no kudos for bearing this message!

Then, on the other hand, innovative members are prone to feel impatient toward those whom they experience as hanging on and holding back. From being eager to get on and experiment with "being church" in fresh ways, they don't want to hear, "Let's stay in respectful relationships with those reluctant to change!" Expect no kudos from them!

To the extent that this metaphor—a bridge pastor—matches your situation, this can be a lonely and misunderstood place to be. It calls for an identity not tied to comfort. It calls for a stance not attached to outcomes. It calls for a few soul friends around you, both within and beyond the congregation, who offer support, understanding, collaboration, and laughter.

I hear this reframe in the words of Václav Havel, the poet, playwright, philosopher, and first president of liberated Czechoslovakia. Let's give him the final word: "Today, many things indicate that we are going through a transitional period when it seems that something is on the way out and something else is painfully being born. It is as if something is crumbling, decaying and exhausting itself, while something else, still indistinct, were rising from the rubble."[1]

With gratitude,
Mahan

Note

[1] Vaclav Havel, "The Search for Meaning in a Global Civilization," (*English Academy Review*, Vol. 16, 1967), 1.

Evolution

Dear Nancy,

This is a different kind of letter. It's about how my theological thinking began to change during my time at Pullen. What began to shift during our working together deepened after retirement. This letter is about my understanding of evolution and its impact on my ministry. I offer it as stimulus for your reflection on the theological underpinnings of pastoral leadership.

For the first half of my ministry, this was the frame: *God and evolution.* They stood at opposite corners. It's not that I didn't believe in evolution. I did. But there was little interaction between my view of God and evolution. The concept of evolution seldom showed up in my sermons or teaching. It was present, but only as a background story, acknowledged but seldom connecting with life experience. Occasionally, if pressed by a creationist, I would defend my view of creation as unfolding over millennia. It was a "soft" belief, one which I knew to be well-documented by contemporary scientists but not crucial for everyday living. Or so I thought at the time. But my curiosity was there all along and never waned.

I do remember imagining the shock of those who lived in the late Middle Ages hearing, "You are no longer the center of the universe!" This startling truth—that the earth revolves around the sun—must have shattered their primal place within a presumed stable, orderly world. It's understandable that into that vacuum science moved triumphantly, solidifying the conviction of our evolving as humans in an evolving universe.

The picture of evolution as compressed into 100 years has fascinated many of us. The Big Bang occurs at the first day of the first year. It is not until sixty-seven years later that our solar system is formed, with us, the human species, appearing around the ninety-ninth year. That leaves the birth of Jesus occurring during the last hours, and the founding of our nation in the last minutes. This is to say, you serve an early, early church.

But for the longest time this was my frame: a fascination with evolution that never was a vital part of my theological worldview…until the reframe. The frame—God *and* evolution—became the reframe—God *in* evolution.

My turn toward this reframe—the evolving universe as metanarrative—
began with Claude Stewart, a nearby professor, whom I asked in 1987 to deepen
my understanding of process theology. My first assignment took me by surprise:
"Read *Report to Greco* by Nikos Kazantzakis." Claude, in his wisdom, didn't want
me to begin with an intellectual discussion of theory. First, he invited me to
experience the evolutionary process, to feel it in my bones, to know it viscerally,
to encounter its throbbing dynamism. He wanted the starting point to be the
awe, power, and beauty of evolution. Kazantzakis's poetic grasp of evolution did
just that:

> Blowing through heaven and earth, and in our hearts and the
> heart of every living thing, is a gigantic breath—a great Cry—
> which we call God. Plant life wished to continue its motionless
> sleep next to stagnant water, but the Cry leaped up within it and
> violently shook its roots: "Away, let go of the earth, walk!" Had
> the tree been able to think and judge, it would have cried, "I
> don't want to. What are you urging me to do! You are demand-
> ing the impossible! But the Cry, without pity, kept shaking its
> roots and shouting, "Away, let go of the earth, walk!"
>
> It shouted in this way for thousands of eons; and lo! As a
> result of desire and struggle, life escaped the motionless tree and
> was liberated.
>
> Animals appeared—worms—making themselves at home
> in water and mud. "We are just fine here," they said. "We have
> peace and security; we're not budging!"
>
> But the terrible Cry hammered itself pitilessly into their
> loins. "Leave the mud, stand up, give birth to your betters!"
>
> "We don't want to! We can't."
>
> "You can't, but I can. Stand up!" ...
>
> And lo! After thousands of eons, man emerged, trembling
> on his still unsolid legs. Man calls in despair, "Where can I go?"
> And the Cry answers, "I am beyond. Stand up!"[1]

This Cry, this pitiless hammering in our loins, the Beyond luring us
forward—don't you feel it at times? You know that fiery mixture of fear and
excitement welling up within, whispering or shouting on occasion, "Wake up.
Leave your comfort zone. Risk. Stand up. Give birth to your betters!"

Your mother felt this Cry. So did my mother. At our births each one heard the Cry. While fearing "I can't do this! This is too hard, too painful!," they heard the counter Cry rising within them: "You can. Let go. Yield to the struggle. Embrace the pain. Don't hold back. Give birth to 'your betters.' Welcome the new life coming through you!"

You felt that Cry when you decided for the first time to stand up on your own two legs. It was a micro-moment of defying fear by choosing the risk of walking over the comfort of crawling. It was the same Cry calling you to courage when you risked preaching your first sermon, or when you vowed "yes" at your ordination, or when in an important relationship you risked rejection for a deeper acceptance and intimacy, or when you took a stand out of integrity in the face of inner voices shouting, "No. Don't do it. We're just fine here. Don't disturb us." Yet you heeded a different voice, and, to your surprise, your self-confidence thickened. The feared catastrophe likely didn't happen. So it is when you "give birth to your betters."

You can almost hear this Cry pounding in the heart of a trapeze artist: the risk of letting go of one bar, feeling the "up in the air" anxious suspension, yet trusting the new bar coming toward you. It's the metaphor I turn to when I think of evolution: the summons to risk failure for a higher stage of growth, to risk discomfort for the sake of integrity, to risk misunderstanding for a more complex, deeper mutuality. It's the Cry, a gigantic breath "blowing through heaven and earth, and in our hearts and in the heart of every living thing," a force we call God and Spirit.

After reading Kazantzakis, I continued to explore the theological understanding of evolution. I have been particularly guided by Franciscan scholar Ilia Delio in her lecturing and in her books, my favorite being *The Unbearable Wholeness of Being: God, Evolution, and the Power of Love*. In Paul's letter to the Romans we hear a similar note in this translation: "All around us we observe a pregnant creation. The difficult time of pain throughout the world are simply birth pangs. But it's not only around us, it's in us. The Spirit of God is arousing us within."[2]

This reframe expanded my perspective in multiple directions. My theological worldview has never been the same since Kazantzakis. Here are some ways my mind turns when looking through the evolution lens.

The back door on my sense of *history* is blown away, opening a long corridor. Our human capacity for transcendence, that sense of being part of Something larger, assumed to be distant, is actually comparably recent. It's recent because we humans are recent.

Creation did not happen; creation is happening. Nothing is ordered, fixed, and stable. Life is dynamic, chaotic, devolving, evolving, ever more complex, demanding ever more collaboration. At our best, we are co-creators with God in an unfinished universe.

Our *planet*, the beautiful blue ball pictured from outer space as whole, undivided, becomes the compelling and essential mythic symbol of our age.

Reality is relational, interconnected, systemic, fluid, ever-evolving on all levels from micro to macro within an expanding universe. Separation is an illusion.

God is active within our evolving creation; our evolving creation is within God (pan-en-theism). God is the Cry, the Lure, the summoning life-force of Love—Love as *eros*, desiring to connect creatively; as *philia*, forming covenant partnerships; and as *agape*, radical self-giving to the "other," the neighbor "as yourself." God is the subject of Love, glowing and active in and through our relationships. We are called to join, align, and participate in this Love.

The *Spirit* is divine Love-in-action. Evolution is Spirit-in-action.

Jesus, life-giver, icon of the fully human, is the divine Cry incarnated, giving body, mind, and soul to this movement toward the fullness of shalom.

Church is those who desire and allow the Love embodied in Jesus to be embodied in them, his body in the world.

Prayer is surrendering to and partnering with this divine movement toward justice and right relationships (shalom), allowing ourselves to be transformed in the process.

Meditation is an inner muscle builder, a repeated practice of letting go the inner noise of anxious mental thoughts, past or future, and falling into the heart space of "belovedness," our true human nature, our deepest identity.

Worship, from a place of awe, is our self-offering to the God movement toward wholeness (shalom).

Hope is standing back, way, way back, far enough to see the vastness of evolution with its repeated patterns of death and resurrection, dying and rising, the Paschal Mystery with its movement toward increasing complexity and collaboration. My hope is in those who hear and heed this summoning Cry, feeling it, exploring it, fearing it, and, over and over again, yielding to its call to "give birth to their betters."

Commitment, from sensing and knowing the evolutionary impulse to create from Love, we choose to participate in this compassion that is wanting to become flesh through our personalities.

I am not proposing determinism or some fairy-headed optimism. Within evolution is devolution, the loss and death of things as part of the process. It just doesn't have the last word.

As I write, our earth is warming at an alarming rate. We humans have yet to control the rate of fossil fuel emissions from our vast manufacturing networks. Since the Industrial Revolution, the world has warmed one degree Celsius. The international Paris climate treaty signed in 2016 is designed to restrict the warming to two degrees. The treaty is not holding, and the chances of succeeding are slim. Even if accomplished, extinctions of tropical reefs and sea-rise of several meters are occurring. At a three-degree rise, most coastal cities will be lost and more extinctions of non-human species will occur. At four degrees, Europe will be in permanent drought as will vast areas of China, India, and the American southwest. At five degrees, human civilization would come to an end.

We experience both the pull of evolution and the force of devolution. Extinctions occur. From self-destructive and earth-destructive behavior, we *homo sapiens* may be next. Yet evolution will not end. The drive that attracts, connects, and creates—the summoning force of evolution—will not end. Death never has the final word. As I am wanting to trust, life keeps coming out of death, a conviction from our faith tradition, my trust in the Cry, and my understanding of evolution.

Recently, some elder friends and I were lamenting the current state of affairs. The conversation bounced around the table. "Democracy is gone. Let's face it. We have an oligarchy, the few with wealth and political power calling the shots," said one friend. Another bemoaned international crises, saying, "I can't stand watching nations implode, with thousands of refugees fleeing for safety. I see no solution." Still another reminded us of our founders' choice, a messy political process over the option of tyranny. He lamented, "Yet now in the last decade people are elected to obstruct the political process as a way to sabotage the other political party."

The chorus of despair continued. After a while I asked my friends, "Well, what gives you hope?" Like a boomerang the question came back, "Well, Mahan, what gives *you* hope?"

I told them about the Cry, the pulse of evolution toward shalom, toward collaboration, toward community. And now I'm telling you.

With gratitude,
Mahan

Notes

[1] Nikos Kazantazakis, *Report to Greco* (London: Faber and Faber, 1973), 291–292.

[2] (Romans 8:22–23, *The Message*) Copyright © 1993, 1994, 1995, 1996, 2000, 2001, 2002. Used by permission of NavPress Publishing Group.

Myths: Redemptive Violence, Redemptive Nonviolence

Dear Nancy,

Seldom does one person in one book change profoundly the way you see life. Yet it was from the impact of one book that I began seeing reality, evil, the sacred, and myself with new eyes. This person is Walter Wink. This book is *Engaging the Powers*.

I'm sure we have talked about this book. I discovered it about the time we began working together in 1992. Since then, I have reread this book about every couple years. It's been that generative. And its intellectual and spiritual challenge is so huge that I'm still trying to internalize its wisdom.

In this letter I have teased out the primary gift: seeing two invisible realities—the domination system, driven and held in place by the myth of redemptive violence; and the domination-free system, the realm of God, relational partnerships embodied in Jesus, his teaching and life. These are two fundamentally incompatible human systems. Two alternatives. Two frames. Two sources of power. Two ways of seeing, being, and living in the world. But one—the domination system—is built on a lie. Violence does not redeem. The other is redemptive, liberating, life-giving, love-releasing. As Christians we live within the tension of both systems. We have a foot in both narratives.

Let a childhood story set the stage. This may be the warmest, most cherished memory I have of my father. The experience is vivid and intimate. Every Monday, Wednesday, and Friday evening from 6:30 to 7:00 was *Lone Ranger* time. Dad would stretch out on the chaise sofa. I sat at its edge with both of us an arm's length from the small bronze radio on the bookshelf. For thirty minutes we would lose ourselves in this bubble of shared imagination. From my seventh to tenth year, this was our weekly ritual.

But I came to discover that more was happening than an intimate father/son moment. From reading Wink I saw this experience with new eyes. Each *Lone Ranger* episode followed the same pattern, a pattern also consistent with the other prominent cartoons of the day like Popeye, Batman, Superman, and Captain Marvel. This same pattern runs through the high-tech games that currently occupy the imagination of our youth.

Note the pattern: The Lone Ranger and Tonto are the good guys pitted against the bad guys. It looks like the bad guys will win until—with about five minutes left in the broadcast—the good guys overturn the threat and vanquish their evil foes. At the end, the Lone Ranger and Tonto ride away victorious, leaving my Dad and me basking in the moral greatness of this "masked man." Similarly, Popeye, protecting Olive against the brute Bluto, would at the last minute pop open the can of spinach, feel the sudden infusion of power, and proceed to pummel his opponent to near death. The heroes save the day. Winning dominates. Good defeats evil. Violence redeems.

Wink makes a bold claim. He builds a case that these seemingly inconsequential childhood stories quietly and profoundly condition us with the prominent spirituality in America. They culturally shape us, as do the major stories of violent conquest we tell about our history and current events. This pervasive, persuasive secular spirituality Wink names the *myth of redemptive violence*.[1]

Consider each word. *Violence* is destructive, overpowering acts that demean the human (or non-human) "other" with the aim of dominating, controlling, or winning, as in winning an argument or winning a war. *Myth* is a worldview or belief or narrative that mirrors a particular view of reality. We all have myths or narratives through which we see the world. The myth of *redemptive* violence is the assumption that violence redeems, violence saves, violence wins, violence deters aggressors, violence solves problems, violence brings peace, violence eradicates evil, and violence is innate and natural. Wink puts them together: the myth of redemptive violence.

In the *Lone Ranger* myth, the Lone Ranger and his sidekick Tonto redeem or save by overpowering the enemy through violence, usually gun violence. They are righteous; the opposition is evil. They are good; the enemy is bad. Within the Lone Ranger, his interior life, there is no sign of ambiguity, no sense of internal contradiction, no indication of guilt, no trace of wrong, no hint of evil. Whatever fear or outrage he feels is projected onto the face of the enemy. The evil is "out there" to be destroyed.

Thus, as a young boy, week in and week out, I tasted the delight in identifying with the good guys, the heroes, the saviors. It was an emotional "hit," an adrenaline rush. My brain was being wired with this story and other similar stories told to me in school and around the dinner table. In my fantasies, I relished the place of feeling righteous, in control, superior, justified, and applauded for doing heroic work. A foundation was being laid. A script was being written that remains to this day a tempting story to embrace as mine.

Walter Wink gave me new eyes in 1992. I began to see this myth of redemptive violence everywhere. I observed it being played out on macro and micro levels: from the *macro* events of forcing democracy (a nonviolent form of government) by violent means in the Middle East or one political party gaining the force to overpower the opposition in their effort to solve national problems, to the *micro* violence of controlling a relationship in the effort to save it or cutting off the conversation to preserve stability or playing the pastor "card" or male "card" to save a desired outcome in a committee meeting.

I kept saying, "There it is. There it is." I could see it at work in so many places: countering murdering by killing murderers; stopping children fighting by spanking them; maintaining control in the home through physical or psychological abuse; establishing security with more guns for citizens; annihilating the evil of terrorism; declaring war on poverty or drugs; lynching black bodies to keep submissive "peace." Even in my writing group of inmates in a maximum prison I saw it. At the moment of their violent act, they were attempting to solve a problem. They were trying to save something vital to them.

I began to see redemptive violence in play within congregational life too. Take a member who becomes oppositional. They start behaving in harmful, manipulative, and dominating ways. That is, they are violent. If I could see it for what is, I might, before I react, ask some Wink-soaked questions: Who or what are they trying to save? What problem are they trying to solve? Is there a gift in their opposition? Answers, after a few moments of reflection, just might open up another way forward.

Nancy, you came to Pullen at the end of my being a target for some fundamentalist Christians in our denomination. I was their enemy. They implemented devious strategies to discredit me—taping my talks without permission, quoting me out of context, mounting a campaign to fire me as an adjunct professor in a nearby seminary, and "dis-fellowshiping" Pullen from the denomination on local, state, and national levels. They were successful on all points.

I happened to be reading Wink during those years. His insight took the edge off my anger and bewilderment. I heard his counsel: "See it. See it for what it is. It's not about you. They don't even know you personally. These persons with the loud voices and direct actions are trying desperately to save, redeem what, in their judgment, is being undermined by you and your ilk. The end—saving their vision of church—justified any violent means. Recognize that you are cancer to the body that must be destroyed. That's what we do with cancer cells. We seek to eliminate them."

This insight did help me carry these turbulent times a little more lightly, not take the accusations so personally, weigh my responses more carefully, and, on my best days, see my enemies with a modicum of understanding, a prelude to forgiving them. We marvel at Jesus's capacity to love and pray for the forgiveness of the very ones killing him. And note his commentary: "for they know not what they are doing." These enemies—a coalition of the military, political, and religious leaders—didn't know that violence would not solve their problem with Jesus. In the long run it never does. Violence provokes more violence.

This is another "sighting." At one point I was wanting to change a staff configuration. You were there, so maybe you remember this effort. It made good sense to me that a part-time person become full time and in the process redefine her focus. Time was short to make this change. I happened to mention this hope of mine to a supportive member of the congregation. Matt, let's call him, immediately became invested in helping me create a strategy for achieving my goal. With a spark in his eyes, he said, "Mahan, let's figure out your allies. Then let's name your opposition." Before I knew it, I was swept up into a strategy to overtake the opposition and "win" what I wanted.

So quickly I was Lone Ranger with Tonto at my side, looking for ways to defeat the opposition. Thankfully, I saw it and caught my eagerness to implement this violent plan of action to save a staff situation. So I backed off and proceeded with a more nonviolent, collaborative process that was a bit long and messy and that yielded a conclusion opposite to my original thinking.

Nancy, a more personal example is our relationship. It took you a while to point out a pattern all too frequent in committee meetings. You would present an idea, a solution to a problem, or a vision of a way forward. But only when I affirmed it did it have traction. Even worse, the committee left feeling the idea was mine, and I left feeling proud, a Lone Ranger kind of pride. You helped me see. But I wonder about all the times my behavior was similarly violent beyond my awareness. I catch myself sometimes, and when I do, I have a choice to make. That's my hope.

This takes me to the last section of his book, where Wink writes openly of his inner work with violence or, as he words it, loving the enemy within. Again, it's about seeing redemptive violence at work, but this time it's about how it works in me—namely, how I do violence to myself in the effort to save myself. The inner voices I hear from the system are consistent: "You don't compare well. You are not strong enough, effective enough. Try harder." These voices are not new. But what is new, thanks to Wink, is the awareness that this violence to myself is an effort to redeem myself. Prodding and provoking and condemning myself are attempts to change myself for the good. In theological language, I am attempting to justify myself, save myself, earn my well-being that we both know is only gift, not achievement.

But Wink takes me even deeper to the work with my privilege. My whiteness, my maleness, my heterosexuality, my Americanism, my economic status—these are all benefits of the system. All of these are structures of privileged dominance. All of these assume separation, ranking, and division. These are the cards I was dealt. Not one of them have I earned, and yet each one advantages me. Privilege is part of the public conversation today in a way it was not when I was pastor. But Wink even then sounded a new note. When I act from supremacy in relationships, I not only violate others; I also violate myself, my soul. My soul, my deepest self, is nonviolent love. My deepest identity is beloved. That's who I am, by God's grace. When I act otherwise, from a position of power over, then I act against myself. I violate my essence.

Let's turn to Jesus. Jesus and his way of relating embodies the domination-free system. Wink gave me not a new Jesus, but a clearer Jesus. As if looking through a camera, he helped me bring Jesus into sharper focus. Jesus drew a clear, red line in the dirt, offering a distinct, full-blown alternative to structures of domination kept in place by redemptive violence. Jesus exposed and countered the assumption that "violence is just the way life works." Jesus was not the first to teach nonviolent living, but he, beyond just teaching, incarnated this power of God at work in the world. He helped us see what a partnership, domination-free reality looks like.

Wink clarified the death of Jesus. Jesus challenged all the props that hold up the system—wealthy over poor, Jews over Samaritans, clean over unclean, men over women, Roman military over citizens, righteous over unrighteous, and other binary in-out, good-bad, over-under relationships. He challenged them all, not primarily with frontal attacks, but by living an alternative way that exposed and undermined the domination systems of his day. And it cost him his life. Those in positions of power had to eliminate this challenge. They had to kill him—or change. Predictably, they chose to execute him, thinking, of course, that this would solve their problem.

Have you ever wondered why the church didn't retain the sharp edges of the Jesus vision? The church couldn't sustain some of his countercultural ways, such as his treatment of women, the marginalized valued, his view of servant leadership, his nonviolent ways of conflict resolution, and his insistence on loving and praying for our enemies. Why did the church water down the message of Jesus? It's because of the entrenched systems of domination. In order for the church to have ongoing life, Jesus had to be tamed. In time, they, and now we, more easily worship Jesus than follow him. The church then and now has to be understood as existing within deeply rooted systems of domination.

Pre-Wink, I was naive about the power of structural, systemic evil. I underestimated the domination system's capacity to seduce, undermine, and neutralize the partnership system of equity and justice. He opened my eyes to its power and preeminence for the past 5,000 years. No wonder its force is largely assumed as the way life must be structured.

So the "way, the truth, and the life" of nonviolent living and nonviolent strategies for social change are relatively new. Wink suggests that this alternative power is about at the stage that the power of electricity was in the days of Marconi and Edison.[2] But, as with electricity, huge advances are happening. We could name examples: the rise of democracy, abolishing slavery and child labor, marriage as partnership, and all the liberation movements in our time—voting rights, women's rights, civil rights, gay rights, children's rights, employment and work rights. Plus, there have been numerous examples of dictatorships dismantled through direct nonviolent actions. Momentum of this movement is increasing. Dare we say that the cutting edge of evolution is change through partnerships of nonviolent love and action?

Wink brings the apostle Paul's metaphor to life and provides a fitting ending of this letter. Paul writes in his letter to the Ephesian church that we struggle not against persons whose worldviews differ from ours. Our deepest struggle is not how to vote out toxic leaders or how to find a better pastor and outmaneuver our opposition. Our struggle is against principalities and powers, translated by Wink as the domination system held in place by the myth of redemptive violence. In the 1960s there was a familiar saying during the civil rights movement: "The problem is not Mr. Charles. It's the Mr. Charles in your mind." Precisely. It's the system in our heads. We live in this system. We breathe in this system. It's the system against which we struggle. To engage and counter the system will meet deep-rooted resistance both from others and within ourselves. This is a hope. We can come to know when the system is talking. We can grow in acknowledging and resisting the system's control of our decisions. We can see and choose the options of mutuality, collaboration, and partnership.

Through Wink's ears I hear Paul warning us: If you are going to struggle against these invisible powers, then any personal willpower, ego strength, and determination is vastly insufficient. You need the whole armor of God to protect you and keep you standing firm. Don't be naive, writes Paul. You are up against aggressive, seductive, effective, winsome forces of power that act from violence believed to solve problems. The armor, he continues to write, is fortified by spiritual "weapons" drawn from the domination-free system, the alternative reality that Jesus fleshed out: belt of truth, breastplate of right/just relationships, shoes of the gospel of peace/shalom, shield of faith/trust, helmet of salvation/wholeness, and sword of the Spirit, God's Word, and praying earnestly as if you could never stop. This is what it takes. This spiritual fortification not only helps you survive in the domination system; it gives you the freedom to live and engage from a core of nonviolent, partnering power. And these spiritual practices are not just individual efforts. Paul is writing to the church in Ephesus. These spiritual practices we cultivate together in community.

The church, if I understand Wink, is the locus where this struggle between these two systems is highlighted. It's where we see both systems. The congregation is where we keep putting on the whole armor of God. It's where we confess complicity. It's where we hone our spiritual "weapons." It's where we face this challenge writ large: How to be *in* the world (*kosmos*, translated by Wink as the domination system) but not subject to its power. How to be in it but not *of* it. How to be *of* this alternative way of partnership.

Nancy, this has been the hardest letter of all to write. Wink's framing the powers, both redemptive violence and redemptive nonviolence, was for me a reframing of my worldview. It's been so consequential that to condense his witness to a letter is impossible. Wink's way of seeing changed my theological and pastoral landscape. I'm a witness inviting you to be one too.

With gratitude,
Mahan

Notes

[1] Walter Wink, *Engaging the Powers* (Minneapolis: Fortress Press, 1992), 13–85.
[2] Ibid., 232.

Establishment to Disestablishment

Dear Nancy,

This bit of practical wisdom from philosopher Sam Keen during my seminary years has stuck to me like Velcro: "A wise person knows what time it is in his/her life and in the life of their times." It's a handy question when mired in a confused place. "Now what time is it in my life? What is it not time for?"

The other part of his question is handmade for leaders—"in the life of their times." Or more pointedly, "What time is it for our congregation in the life of our times?"

In the early 1980s the Canadian theologian Douglas John Hall came to my attention. His way of seeing the church in history became for me both a frame and a reframe. The frame: establishment. The reframe: disestablishment.

With convincing lucidity Hall announced that Christendom is almost over. The 1,500 years of established church prominence in Western civilization is coming toward its end. In Europe the church has clearly already lost its established prominence. In our country, in particular in the South, it has been a more gradual loss of status. Disestablishment is not yet complete.[1]

My journey with the church has mirrored this movement from establishment to disestablishment. Born in 1934, a Knoxville, Tennessee, native growing up during "pre" to "post" World War II years, I experienced the church as *established*. Along with other respected institutions (governmental, legal, educational, medical), the church was visible, prominent, and, from all appearances, permanent. The church seemed to be a dependable trellis, a trustworthy frame that supported the communal vines of morality. In most cases religious identity was inherited, much like skin color or last name or political affiliation. Most everyone in my small world went to a church or synagogue.

Signs of this establishment were conspicuous: church and state, arm in arm in the World War II "war effort"; American flags in places of worship; opening prayer at civic occasions, including football games; "ministerial discounts" for pastors (can you believe that!); only males as pastors; Jews a silent minority; Muslims, Hindus, Buddhists unheard of. After all, I assumed, we were a Christian nation.

Even in seminary years Protestant Christianity was presumed to be the dominant religion nationally and the superior religion globally. Those were the days when a theologian, Reinhold Niebuhr, and a Baptist preacher, Theodore Adams, could make the front page of *Time* magazine.[2] And in my small world, foreign missionaries, intent on winning the world for Christ and establishing congregations much like the ones back home, wore the badges of supreme devotion and honor.

But even then, cracks began appearing in the established church. *The Secular City* by Harvey Cox was for me the announcement of the growing rise of secularism. As graduate students we pondered the meaning of Bonhoeffer's inscrutable phrase, "religionless" Christianity.[3] The "death of God" theologians were even more mystifying.[4] Cropping up here and there were advocates for other worldviews, both religious and nonreligious. Denominational vitality and loyalty were beginning to wane. Even the "renewal" movements of the time felt like efforts to recover something important that had been lost and needed recapturing.

Yet churches were growing, or were expected to, when I assumed my first full-time post as pastor in 1967. Still fueled by the optimism of post-war years, congregations, particularly suburban churches, were growing. Once a person accepted the role as pastor, it was assumed that with effective leadership, the congregation would surely grow larger. Anything less would be failure.

But something was changing that I couldn't see, name, or measure. Underground plates of certainty were shifting. The "foundations were shaking," to borrow Tillich's phrase.[5] I began to feel disoriented.

Along came Douglas John Hall at just the right time. He gave me a sense of the church's position in history. His message: "You have been living and serving the church during the last stage of the church as established and dominant."

This last period of transitional stage is where you and most pastors offer ministry. You serve a church no longer culturally established but yet not totally disestablished. Your church falls somewhere along that continuum from culturally established to culturally disestablished. Hall invites us to step way, way back to see the larger picture. I hear him saying, "Open your eyes. See it! See the evidence all around us. Christianity as it has been in Western civilization is winding down from its privileged status. The mainline church is becoming the sidelined church. We are experiencing the end of Christendom's 1,500 years of high standing and dominance."

During these fifteen centuries, empires, kings, philosophers, and political systems have come and gone. But the church in the West maintained its continuity. While it's true that during these centuries there were always small, alternative faith communities, the larger church never lost its established status. Hall convincingly names the bit-by-bit ending of Christendom while acknowledging its remaining vestiges in places like the Southern states in our country. The fundamentalist takeover of our own denomination (Southern Baptist) in the 1970s and 1980s and the rise of the Religious Right may, in part, be a backlash to this erosion of Christendom.

But this is the word I most treasure from Hall. He is not despairing. He sees birth, not just death. For him we are experiencing the birthing of a different role and shape for church in our society.

This was Hall's gift to me. He reoriented me. He named convincingly the current place of the Western church in history. Hall offered a reframe with a *beginning*, an *end*, and *new life*.

The *beginning* was Emperor Constantine's adoption of Christianity as the official religion of the empire in the fourth century; the *end*, after 1,500 years, is a gradual decline of the church's established position in the West. These two great social transitions mark the history of the Western church. But arising from this ending of Christendom—and this is the good news—are emerging expressions of church that are more flexible, humble, inclusive, and experimental, with new forms of Christ-life and mission in our midst.

Hall invited me to revere establishment, accept disestablishment, and welcome the new that is coming toward us. Lets heed his challenge.

First, revere the long season of establishment. Honor the tradition. Look for the breakthroughs of faith, wisdom, and courage through these years. Note the parts of our past tradition we can either release or build on.

Second, accept disestablishment. Don't just accept with doleful resignation the loss of privileged status. Welcome it. Embrace it. Claim the freedom from its frequent, heavy insistence on certainty and "right" believing. Claim in our historical moment the chance to explore new ways of being church. Engage the challenge of leading a congregation that is positioned on the cusp of such an ending and beginning.

Hall sees the church today as becoming parallel to the church in the first few centuries before Emperor Constantine. These first followers of Jesus were a minority, at times a persecuted minority. These first congregations were feisty, uniquely diverse communities' alternative to the more established institutions of the day. They were living examples of the transforming power of the small, more closely embodying the favorite metaphors of Jesus—yeast, salt, seeds, candlelight, little flock, small cup of water. Jesus was consistently—almost exclusively—about the extraordinary promise coiled within small efforts by those on the margins, in other words, by those disestablished.

Ponder the metaphor of yeast. A small portion of yeast must be prepared and kneaded into the bread repeatedly in order for it to release its transforming power. I take heart when I imagine the church as yeasty communities—small and not so small—doing its transforming work virtually unnoticed.

Hall is suggesting that these favorite metaphors of Jesus are lenses through which we can see the contours of the church emerging.

In this post-Christendom era the church will be measured less by cultural prominence and institutional strength. With that expectation waning, we are in a better position to heed what Hall considers to be the deepest longings of our time: the quest for *moral authenticity*, the quest for *meaningful community*, the quest for *transcendence and mystery*, and the quest *for meaning*.

Nancy, you are a seasoned pastor, not the young pastor you were when we began working together. I am wondering how younger clergy will respond to this letter. They may not have experienced the church established as we did. Whether or not that's true, they serve congregations with members ambivalent about becoming disestablished.

Thanks to you, Douglas John Hall, for your location of the contemporary Western church in history that resonates with what I felt and observed. Your reframing invites a lightness, curiosity, and trust in the Spirit at work in our dying and in our rising. You speak to the question that provokes imagination: What time is it in the life of the church in the life of our times?

And thanks to you, Nancy, and those like you, who serve the church in such a time as this.

With gratitude,
Mahan

Notes

[1] Douglas John Hall, *The End of Christendom and the Future of Christianity* (Eugene, OR: Wipf and Stock Publishers, 2002), 1–18.

[2] Theodore F. Adams, pastor, First Baptist Church, Richmond, Virginia, *Time Magazine* cover, December 5, 1955.

[3] The phrase "religionless Christianity" is found in Dietrich Bonhoeffer's letters from his prison at Tegel, Germany. He critiques the church for insisting on language and forms no longer viable. The post-war (World War II) church must find new language and structures

to convey the Christian message. See Eberhard Bethga's biography, *Bonhoeffer* (New York: Harper Collins, 1979), 104–109.

[4] The death of God theologians represented a range of ideas that attempted to account for the rise of secularity and abandonment of traditional beliefs in God. These thinkers arose to some measure of prominence in the late 1950s and 1960s.

[5] "The shaking of the foundations" is the title of a book of sermons by Paul Tillich (New York: Charles Scribner's Sons, 1948).

Promises

Dear Nancy,

A story opens up this reframe: Martin was an exchange student from Germany. At the end of his year with our family, his parents came for their first visit to our country. After their whirlwind tour of our nation, they ended their vacation with us. I asked Karl, the father, "You've covered a lot of our country, exploring an amazing amount of territory. In all that travel, what surprised you the most?" His answer has never left me: "I'm surprised by all the churches." Karl went on, "It's remarkable. They are everywhere. I'm told that each church is on its own. The members make it happen. Not so in our country. We all pay taxes to support the church even if you don't attend."

His observation had never occurred to me. Even now, I must admit, when I see a church building, I often marvel, like Karl, at the existence of that congregation. You and I pass probably fifteen or so churches each day as we drive through our communities. Has it ever struck you as remarkable that each congregation, whatever the size and flavor, consists of enough people who give and keep promises? That's the glue. When congregants stop keeping their promises, trust erodes, and soon the building is empty with locks on doors to prove it.

This is a truth profound in its simplicity: *All relationships, not just congregations, are held together by the willingness and capacity to make and keep promises.* It's a fragile thread, invisible and essential. Relationships are kept alive by ordinary, simple, everyday promise-making: "I will be home at six. If not, I'll call you." "Agreed. Let's do it." "I'll tell you about it when I get to the office." "Will you give me a ride?" "How about coffee at ten, our usual place. Will that work?" "I forgot. Our meeting was right there on my calendar, but I didn't see it. I'm so sorry. Can we reschedule?"

Everyday acts of making and keeping promises, and of dealing with broken promises, are the bread and butter of living. But they go largely unnoticed. Yet once noticed, the sequence becomes clear: *Promises made*, both small promises and life-defining vows, risk commitment; *promises kept* embody faithfulness, building trust; *promises broken* sow seeds of distrust and, if continued, result in the death of the relationship; *broken promises healed* require some expression of confession and forgiveness. Relationships live or die by promises made and promises kept and broken promises healed.

This insight made its way into my opening statement for wedding ceremonies:

> The wedding ceremony is a joyous occasion, a solemn occasion, and a worshipful occasion. This is a joyous occasion because the possibility of joy from marital life together is one of the deepest we can know on the earth. This is a solemn occasion because the implications of the promises spoken this day will have a ripple effect—for good or for ill—upon countless others down through the years. And this is a worshipful occasion because we worship God, who delights in promises made and promises kept.

This statement seemed adequate until my divorced friend, Leo, attended one of the ceremonies where I was officiating. He offered how he felt alien in the service, like someone looking in from the outside. How could he worship this God, he wondered, with broken pieces of his marital promises in his hands and heart?

So for the next wedding ceremony I added a phrase: "And this is a worshipful occasion because we worship God, who delights in promises made and promises kept and who delights in the healing of broken promises." That seemed satisfactory. I wanted those like Leo to feel the possibility of reconciliation within primary relationships strained and even broken. But Leo continued to feel left out. My words still excluded Leo and those with his life experience who never found any healing in the relationship. In his case, there was no reconciliation with his wife, no friendship, no contact. They had promised faithfulness "till death do us part." For them the relationship was dead.

So I added another phrase to the litany: "and who delights in the healing of those broken by broken covenant promises." You may note that I also added the word *covenant* to deepen the biblical, theological dimension of exchanging promises. Covenants, in contrast to contracts, include the exchanges of promises among humans within the larger covenant of God's promises. We learned in seminary about God's covenant with Israel and new Israel (church) as covenant promises to be with us and for us, even in the pain and consequences of broken promises.

Nancy, I'm wondering if our priority on covenants may be particularly subversive in our day. As computer technology becomes a principle organizer and definer of our lives, I'm asking, "Will there be more relationships without commitment and more connections without covenant? Is this gift from our faith tradition something to cherish and sustain?" These are rhetorical questions, of course, more statements than inquiry. The value of covenants seems at the core of who we are.

The philosopher Hannah Arendt has deepened my understanding. She places side by side both the power of promise and the power of forgiveness. The *capacity to make and keep promises provides islands of security as one faces into an always uncertain future.* And the *capacity to forgive* the consequences of broken promises grants freedom from being held hostage to one's past.[1]

Arendt turns me back to Jesus's most revolutionary word—*forgiveness.* If we don't "get" forgiveness, we don't "get" Jesus. Forgiveness, we know from our pastoral work with relationships, is outrageous, unfair, irrational. It requires a release of our grasp to what was. Yet it's the only force that can break the cycle of retribution, blaming, and resentment. Revolutionary indeed.

Seeing pastoral ministry through the eye of covenant promises—made, kept, broken, forgiven, possibly restored—became for me a major reframe that mattered. In this letter I have already written about my evolution of covenant within the marriage ceremony. Here are a few other examples of covenanting in ministry.

Church membership can be framed explicitly as a covenant. The person promises. The church promises. In private conversation I sometimes added the likelihood of dashed hopes and unmet expectations. I assumed disappointment. So I asked this to be included in the promise: *When the covenant isn't working as expected, will you promise to name the disappointment or failure in the hope of a new, deepened covenant?* To see membership as covenants increases the likelihood that these differences and dissatisfactions, including the ending of the covenants, can be occasions for growth. Even a member leaving in anger is sometimes willing to see their exit in covenant terms. By reviewing the covenant, both parties can acknowledge the good, confess failure and disappointment, call upon forgiveness, and bless the future covenant with another congregation.

To see *staff relationships* in covenant terms is another example. When we worked together on staff, we gave attention to this. It was part of each staff retreat. Looking back, I wish it could have been more intentional and regular. I've seen this attention to covenant work well in a few congregations with whom I worked in retirement. It means spending time making covenant—that is, clarifying expectations, naming assumptions, writing the promises down, and committing to review them periodically. The challenge for me was confronting or allowing myself to be confronted when the promises were broken, even the little ones. For re-covenanting to have integrity, it must include acknowledging the failures, asking for forgiveness, and re-promising. Otherwise, the covenant softens, accountability diminishes, avoidance of conflict sets in with the opportunity for growth forever lost.

I recommend an explicit covenant between *pastor and the elected lay leaders.* While lay leaders and I did talk about mutual expectations in general terms, I would now advocate specificity. Since pastor and laity are called to different but complementary roles of leadership, a covenant can define these roles, establishing an agreement that can be reviewed and modified as needed. This enhances accountability while also granting permission to address broken or unfulfilled promises before they fester and enlarge.

The covenant lens is particularly relevant when addressing *congregational conflict and challenges.* Every congregation has a covenant or mission statement, a stated reason for being. This is the purpose around which a congregation gathers to make promises—the more explicit, the better.

For illustrative purposes, let's assume that some heated differences arise around a budget or church property or personnel behavior. The concept of covenant promises provides a way to frame a conversation that invites faithful listening and creative problem-solving. What are the promises being assumed about this conversation? What process are we agreeing to follow? What light from our mission statement might inform this conversation? In other words, how will we proceed in light of our covenant promises to each other and God?

It makes a difference in how difficult conversations are framed. Take the topics of racism, sexism, or LGBTQ persons in our life and life together. It makes a difference to define these often heated conflicts in covenant terms: How will we be in covenant relationship with those of another gender, race, or sexual orientation? To define any ethical challenge as an issue is to invite polarized reactions. It removes us from the hard work of relationships. Racism is not an issue. Neither are the other examples of difference. It's about how will we be in relationship. To frame these "isms" of injustice in terms of relationships invites a different conversation.

I found it crucial, particularly in stressful situations, not to proceed until the agreements (covenants) around process are clear and affirmed. We can draw intentionally from this part of our biblical narrative. The language of covenant promises provides a theological and ethical framework for proceeding with highly charged situations. Covenants are the containers for difficult speech and collective discernment.

All during my preparation for ministry, the word *covenant* was bandied about with familiarity. Only later did I come to see how radical it is. And how practical. All relationships can be viewed in covenantal terms. It's the gospel in a nutshell: promise-making (risking commitment), promise-keeping (trust), confronting broken promises in the hope of re-covenanting (reconciliation), and the healing grace offered to those broken by broken promises (confession/forgiveness).

Arendt helped me sharpen this gospel truth in these two ways: one, promise-making and promise-keeping provide communities of trust, hope, and love for facing into an uncertain future; and two, the radical giving and receiving of forgiveness grants the freedom to release the hold of brokenness from our past.

Nancy, this may be one of the most practical tools we have that comes right from the heart of our faith story. My awakening to its power came from such an unlikely source—a German visitor to our country. But once grasped, it became a lens through which I could see all pastoral ministry, not to mention all my life in relationships. Maybe Hannah Arendt was not overstating her case: "Against the unpredictably, against the chaotic uncertainties of the future, the remedy lies in the ability to make and keep promises."[2]

I'm aware, as I write this letter, of my appreciation for the covenant of faithfulness we have shared over the years. Our son died suddenly a few years ago. When you heard about it, you got in the car and drove to Asheville to be with us for two hours. Then you drove back the almost five-hour trip to Raleigh. In that brief moment through you I experienced the power of covenant love (*chesed*).

With gratitude,
Mahan

Notes

[1] d'Entreves, Maurizo, "Hannah Arendt," the *Stanford Encyclopedia of Philosophy* (2019 edition, fall, 2019).

Arendt critiques the role of contemplation in Platonism, Stoicism and Christianity for elevating and distancing contemplation from the entanglements and frustrations of active life. Arendt's proposal by contrast, calls for developing the capacity of forgiving and the faculty of promising. Forgiving enables us to come to terms with the past and liberates us to some extent from the burden of irreversibility. Without being forgiven we would not be released from the consequences of what we have done; without being bound to the fulfillment of promises, we would never be able to keep our identities.

[2] Ibid.

Ritual Liminal Space

Dear Nancy,

You have heard me say that the potential power of rituals, more than any other one factor, accounted for my return to congregational leadership. From the sidelines, off the "playing field" for ten years, I observed that rituals were the heart and soul of church ministry. I missed creating and leading them.

We are ritual-making animals. We can't function without them. Take any sporting event. The performance is framed within familiar, repeated, predictable patterns, songs, and symbols, both verbal and nonverbal. The Super Bowl may be our most public ritual. The same ritual behavior marks any patriotic event, such as an inauguration or Fourth of July celebrations. And let's take note that for decades the most contentious issue in public and church life has been over a ritual that celebrates same-sex marriage. Or dive deep into any family and you discover rituals around eating, celebrating holidays, birthdays, and anniversaries. We are ritual-making animals.

Rituals particularly cluster around life's nodal events: *birth*—baby shower, the passing of cigars, baby announcements, and perhaps infant baptism or child dedication; *initiation into adulthood*—joining the army, walking the Appalachian Trail, a driver's license, and perhaps baptism, confirmation, or bar/bat mitzvah; *marriage*—weddings in a home or outdoor setting and perhaps in a sacred place of worship; *death*—gatherings for storytelling, brief words at a graveside and perhaps in an institutional place of worship.

Why rituals? What do they do? Why are some rituals empowering and others perfunctory, anemic, and even boring?

I returned to parish ministry in 1983 with a reframe that mattered. This new pair of glasses came from the early tribal wisdom of "initiation" or "rite of passage" available to us from the research by anthropologists such as Arnold Van Gennep and Victor Turner.

A rite of passage calls for three stages: *separation...open space* in which serious challenge occurs...*returning* transformed. Victor Turner named the in-between period of challenge as "liminal space." *Limen* is Latin for "threshold." They observed young males being separated from their mothers, taken by older males across a "threshold" into an open, unknown space where their capacity for manhood is tested. Then they return to the village, crossing back over the "threshold" no longer as boys but as men, ready now to pick up adult privileges and responsibilities.[1]

This is what pastors do. We welcome others into liminal spaces where trans-formative possibilities are opened. We invite them to stay long enough to engage the essential soul questions: What's going on in my life? What am I learning? To what am I being drawn? Of what must I let go? How will I live? What am I for? Then, after a period of time, they leave that liminal space. They pass back across a threshold, returning to their more familiar, ordinary lives. But in some measure they return as different persons.

I'm raising with you the question following: What if we saw our work in two ways—as creating liminal spaces and, at other times, as naming the liminal spaces *already* created by life circumstances? Let's look at our ministry through the perspective of liminal space provided by rituals.

Take *corporate worship*. In public worship, as leader, I see you creating liminal space. Congregants, by walking through an entrance into the church building, are crossing a threshold, a *limen*. Ideally, they are leaving behind the preoc-cupations of their ordinary, day-to-day lives. They are welcomed into another kind of space, liminal space, designed for reflection on their lives in relationship with God, others, and the world. For an hour or so, the phone doesn't ring, no computer screen confronts them, and no external appeals beg for attention. Congregants settle down into a sanctuary, a safe container with clear boundaries in which they experience various pointers to the presence of the Sacred in their lives and life together.

In this liminal space you and other leaders, as liturgical guides, provide an array of symbols—written, sung, seen, spoken, silent, embodied—that kindle sacred experience. In this safe environment each person is invited to ponder the meaning of their lives, who they are, and what they are about.

Then, after this service of worship, congregants cross back over the threshold, back to their ordinary lives—but not as the same persons who came to worship. No one leaves as the identical person who entered. To be in a safe, contained space with others who are also engaging essential questions is invariably trans-formative. It has to be. To some degree worshipers reenter their familiar lives changed.

If I were a pastor again, I would mark these thresholds more clearly and sensitively. It's so difficult, given the pace of our lives, to leave behind the agendas pressing on our minds. Without a conscious, intentional crossing and returning, the space between will be neither liminal nor transformative.

Or consider how you preside at *funerals or memorial services*. In your role you are not only creating liminal space; you are also naming the liminal space that the grieving family and friends are *already* experiencing. Framing the event as safe, liminal space is the gift. For a brief but "full *kairos*" time, family and friends leave their normal lives and cross a threshold into a numinous place where the meaning of life and death is engaged in intense, profound ways. Then, following this extraordinary time, everyone returns to their ordinary lives, but not as the same persons. Within the protected place of a funeral or memorial service, you and I not only review our relationship with a loved one's life and death. We also, at the same time, are reflecting on our own life and death. No one can go through this communal experience and not be affected deeply.

Similarly, leading *weddings* in sacred places is also about creating liminal space. It's so obvious: The individuals, engaged to be married, traditionally enter the liminal space (sanctuary) from separate directions, meeting at the altar before the priest/pastor. Within this holy space they ritualize their union, to be broken only by death (whether relational or physical death). Then they exit together down the aisle, across the threshold, back into the community, no longer as separate persons but as a new unit, a couple, a family. Transformation has occurred, visible and irrefutable.

In *pastoral care*, the dual aspects of creating liminal space and naming a crisis as liminal are ways to see this ministry. It's what pastoral care is.

On one hand, you create sacred space. There is the crossing of a threshold— whether a door to your office or door to a home or coming from the outside and sitting down at a table. You invite the person or family into an out-of-the-ordinary separate place for conversation and perhaps prayer. Within this secure, protected, and confidential space, the unknown occurs. Free from the fear of judgment, life is shared, questions are raised, healing is invited, decisions are made. Then, with the time completed, persons cross back over the threshold, returning to their ordinary lives but somewhat different, somewhat changed.

On the other hand, in the midst of a crisis, some people may be in liminal space and not know it. The crisis thrusts them out of the ordinary to a place where the primary questions of identity and meaning are raised in bold relief. In these instances you help them frame their disruptive experience as liminal, full of testing, questions, and potential significance.

Consider a person grieving the loss of a job held for decades, or a marriage broken after many years, or the loss of health not to be regained, or the death of a loved one. *The grieving itself is liminal space.* A person is propelled into new territory. Suddenly, their lives feel extraordinary. Their hearts are broken open, their mind confused, their will paralyzed. The suffering, not to be denied or even relieved, can be a portal to deeper soul experiences of knowing. It's the in-between place, the liminal space, where new questions can be engaged and old ways relinquished.

Pastoral care has these two dimensions: We regularly invite people into liminal space; at other times, we invite them to see that they are already in liminal space. In both instances we seek to provide a caring presence within these boundaries of extraordinary time.

Even in our role of *managers* and *leaders* of the congregation, we offer liminal space. That's what the opening prayer or opening statement of a committee or business meeting is about. You are saying, "This meeting occurs in a sacred space. We gather as disciples to discern the path of Jesus and sense of Spirit's guidance as best we can." You are inviting them to leave behind their ordinary "business as usual" assumptions, to cross that threshold into *business as worship*. Then, at some point, the meeting will end, some summary stated and benediction offered before members recross the threshold returning to their various individual worlds. Changes in the life of the congregation have occurred in perceptible or imperceptible ways.

It was Victor Turner, Arnold Van Gennep, and conversations with my friend Dick Hester that helped me see the connection between the early human rites of passage and our current multiple rites of passage within congregational life. The sense of urgency I feel is named by theologian Tom Driver: "To lose ritual is to lose the way. It is a condition not only painful and pathetic but also dangerous.... As for the whole society, sooner or later, it will find rituals again.... Rituals have much to do with our fate."[2]

Nancy, you lead the ritual life of Pullen with reverent care and skill. We shared this role for six years, and now, on occasion, I have experienced your ritual leadership during these years of my retirement. May this understanding of liminal space deepen this gift you so effectively offer.

With gratitude,
Mahan

Notes

¹ Stephen Bigger, *"Victor Turner, Liminality, and Cultural Performance*s," a review article of "Victor Turner and Contemporary Performances," edited by Graham St. John (New York and Oxford: Berghahn Books, 2008).

Victor Turner (1920-1983) was an anthropologist deeply concerned with rituals, regarding them as social drama that is transformative. He drew on the work of Arnold van Gennep's concept of "rites of passage" among indiginous tribes. Turner focussed on the concept of limen, meaning "threshold," and hence the term liminality within life transitions.

² Tom Driver, *Liberating Rites: Understanding the Transformation Power of Ritual* (Boulder, CO: Westview Press, 1998), 4.

Collegial Friends

Dear Nancy,

I referenced in a previous letter the isolation from being "set apart" that comes with ordination. That letter, the first one in this section, was about being "symbolic exemplars"—that is, being signs of More Than We Are, pointers to life lived from God's compassion. Furthermore, we are to be *examples* of what that love looks like. And beneath all these expectations we know ourselves as human, so very, very human.

Nancy, it's that set apart difference I want to address in this letter. What do we do with it? How do we handle the difference that wants to breed isolation?

After ordination every relationship is colored, sometimes greatly, sometimes slightly. Even strangers or neighbors, not to mention friends and family, see you differently. Projections—sometimes positive, sometimes negative—are laid on you that reflect a person's prior experiences with God, church, other clergy, and with you as well. These projections come with the job.

You know this truth. You could readily pull up an example. This is one of mine: A parishioner and I met to play a round of golf on a particularly clear, crisp fall day. At the clubhouse a friend of his asks to join us. So the three of us proceed to play golf, and to enjoy the banter between us, which included some risqué jokes from my friend's friend, Fred.

At about the fourteenth fairway, Fred and I are walking together when he asks, "By the way, Mahan, what do you do?" I hesitate, as you do in those situations. Do I tell him or not? I told him, "I'm a pastor. I'm Jim's pastor."

Fred's golf game was never the same for the remaining holes. Neither was he. He lost his spontaneity. He lost his humor. The next day Fred accosted Jim, "Why didn't you tell me he is a preacher?" To be set apart is to be different. To be different can be isolating.

I decided early on that there are two kinds of pastors and priests: those who conclude, "It's up to me. I like it this way"; and those who say, "I cannot do this apart from a few deep friendships with those who 'get ' pastoral ministry." The church historian Martin Marty made this startling comment in his book on friendship: "We have friends, we are friends in order that we do not get killed."[1]

This second kind of pastor similarly declares, "Without friends, this work could kill my spirit, take my soul."

Pastors in the first group are on their own in giving shape to their work. Everything's up to them. It's up to them to find the resources to help them interpret the gospel, read the "signs" of our time in history, intuit feedback, determine their use of time, judge appropriate responses to congregational crises, establish practices of self-care, worship while leading in worship, and integrate the learning from the plethora of resources available to them. This multilayered work is for them to understand, integrate, and deliver. The pastors I know who fit this category are usually competent and confident. Their positive contributions are without question.

I am in the second group of pastors. The depth of isolation of being a pastor came as a surprise to me. I understand the pastor who said on the way out of parish ministry, "The loneliness has consumed me." While I'm slightly on the extroverted side of the Myers-Briggs Indicator, what I am talking about here goes beyond introversion or extroversion preferences. Simply put, this is about being *out of role and in relationships with a few collegial friends who understand the role.* That's it in a nutshell. Note the critical distinction: being both out of role *and* with persons, likely other pastors, who know the role in all its promise and complexity.

You knew when we started working together about my loyalty to a group of colleagues. I doubt if you know the backstory.

This reframe has a clear origin. At the time I was on the staff of the Department of Pastoral Care at North Carolina Baptist Hospitals, Winston-Salem, North Carolina. A strong program of clinical pastoral education (CPE) had developed over many years. I am not a CPE supervisor, but I was an active participant in this model of education. I found it remarkable, sometimes magical. It's a small community of clergy peers committed to each other's mutual learning under skilled facilitation. During those ten years I kept asking, "Why is this model reserved only for preparation in the practice of pastoral ministry? Why is it not the way of doing pastoral ministry?" The question, never answered to my satisfaction, wouldn't leave me alone.

I took this question with me when, in 1983, I moved from being a director of pastoral care in a hospital setting to being a pastor again. The immediate contrast was striking. In my former role the boundaries and accountability were clear. Not so in my new role. At first I reveled in the freedom to construct my own life in ministry, but soon unspoken agreements and unnamed expectations had me scrambling for a clearer role definition. The reality set in: I am on my own. It is up to me, within broad limits, both to define and to nourish my identity as pastor of this congregation.

But the question of collegial community was still with me. I knew I could not do this work alone. So I joined a circle of friends, a small group of men who had been meeting for over ten years. For two hours every other week we gifted each other with an acceptance close to unconditional. It was a container I needed. With these friends I found support for my life—but less so for my life as pastor.

I needed more. I wanted to be with pastor friends who could focus with me on our efforts at priestly and prophetic leadership. The question was still alive from my years with CPE: Could some variation of this collegial learning be possible in parish ministry? I began the search for other pastors who might be interested in this experiment. After a year or so, I sent this letter to a circle of clergy friends:

> *I fear we have internalized the hallmark of our American culture— individualism. For all our talk about communion and indeed for all our efforts in building community with others, we tend to craft our work by ourselves. What Alexis de Tocqueville said of our forebears in democracy in America could be said of us: "They form the habit of thinking of themselves in isolation and imagine that their whole destiny is in their hands."[2]*
>
> *Instead of continuing like this, I wonder if you would be interested in being a part of a clergy Sabbath day—a time to nurture our souls with colleague-friends; a time of learning from each other and enjoying each other; a time to return to our first love, God; a time to be reminded that the ministry of the church belongs to God and not to us.*

Three pastors responded. Another joined us later. For several years we set aside each Wednesday as a Sabbath day for silence, prayer, conversation about our work, rest, laughter, walking in the woods, and celebrating Eucharist. Never in my years as pastor have I felt so balanced between inner work and outer work, contemplation and action, play and work, self-care and self-giving. The five of us had each other to tease apart our tangled ministries. Together we reflected, played, prayed, and learned from each other in ways that yielded new energy, clarities, and encouragements each week.

Yet, over time, the full day became a half-day, then an occasional half-day, and finally no day at all. Our clergy Sabbaths, like sandcastles, gave way to wave after wave of pressing congregational needs. This fragile container of sacred space cracked and finally crumbled after three years or so.

Absent was a clear covenant among us that might have withstood the pull of competing commitments, both from church, family, and within. Absent was a covenant with church leaders who would support and appreciate this expression of vocational self-care. Also absent was a facilitator who might have made a difference. Although we felt the Sabbath day's value, we stopped short of declaring that this ingredient in our ministry—a few pastors committed to mutual nurture, collaboration, and accountability—was nonnegotiable.

The possibility of some form of collegial community stayed alive within me until retirement. In 1998 I retired a bit early at sixty-three in order to continue the experiment. And I have. During these two decades of retirement, I have tested this hypothesis of collegial communities that I came to name AnamCara, Celtic for "soul friend." This was my working definition: *AnamCara is a network of small collegial circles of five to eight clergy leaders of congregations who meet regularly to offer mutual nurture, collaboration, and accountability in their practices of theological reflection, leadership, and soul care.*

The experiments took different forms. Thanks to a Lilly grant, I organized and either led or co-led four ecumenical, interfaith clergy groups, each of eight to ten participants, who met in retreat settings regularly (monthly or bimonthly) for either a year or eighteen months. I was consultant to three other clergy groups. For twelve years I have led a group of Episcopal clergy who still meet monthly for three hours. In total I have worked with over sixty clergy leaders of congregations.

My underlying question in forming these collegial groups was this: Will these clergy leaders complete this way of practicing ministry saying, "This has been another valuable continuing education experience, thank you very much"? Or will they say, "Being in some expression of collegial community must be incorporated in the way I offer ministry"? In other words, will they regard the experience as an educational "add on," or will they see and embrace this other way of being in ministry?

A minority, about twenty-five of the sixty, continued to commit to an ongoing community of peers. Briefly, this is what I learned:

• Honor the resistance; respect the courage required to risk. The vulnerability is twofold: trusting a few others with our personal story; and even more fearful, trusting colleagues with a close look at our pastoral leadership.

- A person or two is needed to recruit and organize this possibility.
- A facilitator, though not always possible, frees the pastors to be completely out of the leadership role. Some groups do well with shared leadership.
- Pastors are more willing to participate fully if the facilitator has had the experience of pastoral leadership.
- These small communities are a *radical* alternative to the deeply internalized individualism in our culture. They are prophetic in that sense.
- Once trust is felt, the sharing among these collegial friends becomes remarkably honest, nourishing, and generative. The hunger for such sharing is deep and just under the surface.
- Ecumenical groups of clergy, with their commonality of serving congregations, offer the richness of differing traditions.
- To be led in worship within such an intimate community is an experience pastors seldom enjoy.

In 2009 this vision was published as *AnamCara: Collegial Clergy Communities.*

Today I've noticed even more creative ways that clergy are in community together. I know of two pastor groups that meet online weekly and face-to-face a couple times annually. These pastors are vitally involved in supporting and resourcing each other's ministries in ways that exceed my efforts in retirement.

The form will vary. No one structure will embody this need. The core to the variety of forms remains the same: pastors committed to peer relationships where they are out of role with those who know the role. Parker Palmer's challenge to teachers could well include pastors: "The growth of any craft depends on shared practice and honest dialogue among the people who do it."[3] *How* this happens is marvelously creative and diverse. *That* this happens is a requisite.

Early into our vocation, I discovered that the service of ordination speaks truth. We *are* set apart. From it we experience difference. Difference invites isolation. This isolation I discovered to be a gift. It's gifted me with the need to seek and find peer soul friendships, both for myself and others. It provoked a reframe that mattered.

With gratitude,
Mahan

Notes

[1] Martin Marty, *Friendship* (Allen, TX: Argus Communications, 1980), 7, 8, 11, 14.

[2] Alexis de Tocqueville, *Democracy in America*, quoted in "Alexis de Tocqueville on Individualism," Saint John's, The Laughing Agave, December 17, 2009.

Tocqueville, a French lawyer, in 1831 traveled throughout American critiquing our nation's half century experiment in democracy.

[3] Parker Palmer, *The Courage to Teach* (San Francisco, CA: Jose-Bass, 1998), 149.

On Time

Dear Nancy,

Let's tackle a topic often in our conversation. How do we structure our time? With pastors in my clergy groups, I have consistently engaged them around their relationship with time. Abraham Heschel may be right: Our greatest challenge is gaining a foothold in time.[1]

It's a unique challenge for us. As pastors we have time in our hands. Not a stethoscope. Not prescriptions or checks to write. No goods to sell. No papers to hold and grade. No maps to consult. We have time—time to show up, listen, speak, ask questions, bless, and invite. Presence in time is what we have to offer.

Nancy, I have no idea about your current relationship with time. You have your well-established patterns by now. My thoughts may be more useful to a reader starting out in our work.

I imagine Pullen saying to you as it did to me: "We free you from having to spend all of your time at work earning money. We are buying your time to lead us." Then, with no clear expectations, virtually no structure or supervision, no schedules offered, they walk away trusting your use, not abuse, of this time given. It's an awesome trust; it's a burdensome freedom.

You know this about me. You've watched me up close. Time—my relationship to it—was the blessing and bane of my pastoral ministry. I loved the freedom of choice; I felt the burden of its up-to-me stewardship.

A pastor whom you and I both know was describing his thirteen-hour Sunday: the early review of his sermon; leading worship, including preaching; a pastoral response to a family crisis; a late-afternoon committee meeting; a hospital visit; and then another meeting at the church that evening. Most disturbing was that while driving home after a long day, his mind was still working, thinking of things not done and people not seen. "Always more, no endings, never enough," he said out loud to himself. Later, he left our vocation, in large part, he said, "for lack of time."

Granted, such long hours are typical for other workers caught up in a job with high expectations, either self-imposed or imposed by others. Thirteen-hour days are not so extraordinary. We all live and work in an environment that applauds overfunctioning. "Not enough time" is a refrain sung by most adults I know.

But (and this may surprise you) for pastors the issue is not about having enough time. It looks that way. It feels that way. But insufficient time is not the problem. The truth is, we have time. That's what we have. Time is the gift that awaits us each weekday morning. It is ours to fill, to spend.

This is the way I see the unspoken, functional covenant between pastor and congregation. It goes something like this:

> We set you apart (ordination) to lead alongside and with us from a different angle. We give you time to understand, define, and offer yourself in the role of pastoral leader. We free you from some, if not all, obligations to earn a salary outside your need to fulfill your calling. We make it possible for you to have time to study, reflect, visit, pray, and be present in ways that nourish your season with us as pastoral leader.

Note the freedom. Let's acknowledge up front the uncommon freedom we have as pastors. Yes, it can be a burdensome freedom, but it is freedom nevertheless. Most laborers, including professionals, have limited to no control over their schedules. Their time is carefully measured, sometimes in fifteen-minute increments. Most workers adapt to schedules largely set for them by others. Not so with us. We have a radical freedom of choice.

This difference I felt keenly when I moved from being a director of a department within a medical center to becoming the pastor of a local congregation again. In my hospital context my work schedule had structure—office hours from 8:00-5:00 Monday to Friday, some standing committees, one boss, with weekends usually free. I could still overfunction, but I knew when I was working beyond the agreed-upon boundaries.

In contrast, the congregation offers minimal structure, vague and conflicting expectations, and fluid boundaries. Apart from Sunday morning worship and a few fixed committees, we pastors are on our own to figure out our best use of time. Unless the misuse of time is flagrant, we are left as our own "boss" when it comes to time-management. It's up to you. It was up to me.

That's my first preliminary point: *We are given time along with the freedom and responsibility to invest it.* A second point I want to make before I name the reframe is this: *We are employed by people who don't understand our job.*

I'm not complaining or blaming, mind you. I am naming a lack of understanding that comes with our profession. And for good reason. Most of our work is invisible to the congregation that employs us. How could it be otherwise when much of pastoral ministry is private? For instance, most lay members seem surprised to learn that preparation for leading a worship service, including crafting a sermon, usually requires at least twelve hours. And how would members know that a funeral service takes an additional six to eight hours of pastoral care, preparation, and leadership of the service? And there is the care we give to individuals and families that must be appropriately confidential. I don't fault the congregation for not understanding our work life.

Formally, in some situations, congregational members are not the employer. For instance, in the Methodist system the pastor is appointed. But *functionally*, I'm assuming that in all parishes the power that allows us to minister belongs to the people. If congregational expectations of the clergy are not met, then it is only a matter of time before the bishop or superintendent or congregational leaders say, "We think it is time for you to move on. The match is no longer a good one. It's not working." Functionally, the congregation is our employer.

Furthermore, with each "employer" (member) a pastor has a slightly different contract, a difference in large part unacknowledged. For example, some members insist on certain standards in liturgical leadership, especially preaching, yet seem less demanding in other areas. Others, however, expect availability and effectiveness in pastoral care. These members can tolerate less quality in worship leadership. Still others look for efficient management. Above all else they expect effective oversight of the staff, budget, programs, and building. A few members give top priority to pastoral leadership in the community, expecting their pastor to be a connecting link between congregational resources and community challenges.

I sound like I'm complaining, but I am not. Members do not intentionally participate in these competing pulls on your time and energy. These overlapping member-pastor contracts are expectations that live beneath congregational awareness and only occasionally surface in conversation.

This is the nature of our work. We offer ourselves in the midst of competing contracts, unconscious assumptions, and unnamed expectations. Our vocation is not for those who require detailed agreements, tight structure, and precise boundaries. Our work requires a deep capacity to live with ambiguity. To the extent that all of this is true, we are left with a daunting responsibility. Our relationship to time is left up to us.

Now, to my point. This is the reframe that mattered to me: *giving top priority to prioritizing my calling in order to prioritize my time.* This may sound backwards.

I'm suggesting that we take time, the time needed, to prioritize the focus of our ministry as prerequisite to making decisions about our use of time.

The place to start is not a "to-do" list for the day. That's too late. The "to-do" list comes last, not first. To begin with a list of what to do today leaves us vulnerable to the immediate, pressing, short-term needs. Left out of the list would be the larger arc of our calling.

Nancy, what I am about to write won't surprise you. But it may feel very structured to others, perhaps compulsive. This was my attempt for some control over my use of time. I loved the freedom to sail in ministry, but I missed a rudder. What follows is my effort to feel some rudder beneath me. For any reader, take what's useful and discard the rest.

This was my way of working with the time that felt like a blank check.

My first focus was self-definition. The ongoing defining of call precedes and informs defining the use of time. I know this takes time, a block of time, possibly a day retreat periodically. Every so often I would sit down before a set of questions that fell into three different contexts from macro to micro perspectives: *church and world*, *congregation*, and *personal life*. Ronald Heifitz calls this "getting to the balcony overlooking your work,"[2] which I referenced in another letter. This is the greatest failing, in his opinion, of current leaders.

Context: *church and world*. What's the call of God to the church in our moment in history? Within our time in American culture, what is the prime purpose of the church? How does our perception of our local community shape the church's witness? What resources, including interpreters of our time, will I turn to for reflections about the church in the world?

Context: *congregation*. With our congregation in its current situation, what am I called to give? What is being asked of me? Where do my gifts and the needs of the congregation meet? What time is it in our congregation's life and mission? With what excitements in the congregation do I need to align?

Context: *personal life*. Is my soul still alive in this role? What's coming alive in me? Where's the gladness? Where's the sadness? Am I doing this work wholeheartedly? If not, why not?

This story about poet David Whyte speaks to "wholeheartedness." Whyte writes about the time he was director of a nonprofit agency and feeling worn down to the bone. He was weary in spirit when he joined Benedictine monk Brother David Steindl-Rast for their regular reading of Rainer Rilke's poetry. "Brother David, tell me about exhaustion," he began. "You know," Steindl-Rast says, "that the antidote to exhaustion is not necessarily rest? The antidote to exhaustion is *wholeheartedness.*"[3]

That's the question I am suggesting. It's to spend time, on occasion, to step back and examine your "heart" for this work. Are we wholehearted? Our preferred language might be: Where are we with our "call," our reason for being in this work? From these reflections, priorities will guide our best use of time.

The hard part is valuing and finding blocks of "balcony" time. No one will require this of you. You must do it yourself.

But it is all the better if this discernment can include others—in particular, close friends, colleagues, congregational leaders, and maybe at times the congregation itself. They join you in living the questions of calling that invites a level of partnership in the process. Nancy, this may remind you of our staff retreats. This big picture work is what we attempted then.

Finally, I came to the daily to-do list. Each day for around ten or so minutes, with the priorities before me, I asked, "Given what is clearer about the church and world, the congregation and myself, *what is the best use of my time* for this day? For the rest of this week?" If I spent a few minutes with that question, I could enter the day with a measure of clarity. Of course, unexpected interruptions, the "bread and butter" of ministry, would occur. But with my focus for the day in place, I was more likely to respond with flexibility to the events coming toward me. I had a frame. My intention was clear. I had a basis for "yes" and "no."

And now a last word. Everything will work against what I have suggested. Sabotage awaits any effort to claim the time for prioritizing your call as prelude to prioritizing your time. You hear the resistance in our questions: Where will I find the time to work with my call and time? Who cares enough to ask, to understand, to support this effort? Can I face the conflict that such clarity of "yes" and "no" will bring?

I assume that you and other readers of these letters will feel fortunate to be given time with few strings attached. That's the gift. The challenge in that gift is what I have tried to unpack. How do you steward this gift *from* your congregation *for* your congregation and *for* yourself and family? This reframe mattered: *to define our fluid call into priorities that inform our daily use of time.*

Nancy, already you have been a pastor longer than I was. And you are still at it. You have your ways of stewarding time. In one of our phone calls, I'll try to remember to raise this question.

With gratitude,
Mahan

Notes

1 Abraham Heschel, *The Sabbath* (New York: Noonday Press, 1951), 3–10.
Heschel distinguishes Judaism as a religion of sacred time, not space.
2 Heifetz and Linsky, *Leadership on the Line*, 51–74.
3 David Whyte, *Crossing the Unknown Sea: Work as a Pilgrimage of Identity* (New York:
Riverside Books, 2001), 132.

God Hates Visionary Dreaming

Dear Nancy,

I know precisely when and where I first read these words, the title of this letter: "God Hates Visionary Dreaming." It was a colorful, cool autumn day, September 1972. I was sitting on a red bench overlooking a lake with the Blue Ridge Mountains in the distance, reading Dietrich Bonhoeffer's classic *Life Together*.

A few weeks prior, in mid-August, I had resigned from Ravensworth Baptist Church in northern Virginia with future employment uncertain. No new ministry to begin. No plans beyond these winter months in Virginia's Shenandoah Valley on a vacant summer camp offered to us by a friend. I have referenced this pivotal story elsewhere in these letters.

With the difficult transition behind our family of six, I now had the space and time to ponder, "What happened? What really happened, particularly within me? What precipitated such an unexpected ending of my first full-time effort as pastor?" For the first time I was in a position to focus more directly on these questions.

As the questions were beginning to become clearer, I turned to reread *Life Together*, Bonhoeffer's reflections on the alternative seminary he started. I was ill-prepared for his words: "God hates visionary dreaming."[1] They leapt off the page, pulling back the curtains on a truth I could not deny. "That's what happened," I remember telling myself. "That's it!"

Nancy, you know me well. I am a dreamer. I love visions of possibilities. It's a part of me I value as a gift. On the Myers-Briggs Indicator the marker most extreme for me is "intuitive." In another letter to you, I advocated for clarity of purpose, mission or vision in a time in our history that demands experimenting with new structures and programs. I quote with favor, as you have, the familiar proverb, "Where there is no vision, the people perish." (Prov 29:18). And haven't you, along with the readers who join us, been captured by God's dream of shalom, as was Bonhoeffer?

Joining God's dream was not Bonhoeffer's concern. Instead, his was writing about our *attachment* to a visionary dream above all else, a form of idolatry. He is naming the peril of overinvesting in an ideal that hardens into a "have to."

With his superlative "God hates," he is trying to get our attention. For sure he got mine.

Bonhoeffer proceeds to trace the danger of visionary dreaming:

> The man who fashions a visionary ideal of community demands that it be realized by God, by others, and by himself…. He who loves his dream of a community more than the Christian community itself becomes a destroyer of the latter, even though his personal intentions may be ever so honest and earnest and sacrificial…. When his ideal picture is destroyed…he becomes, first an accuser of his brethren, then an accuser of God, and finally, the despairing accuser of himself.[2]

I see in this warning both a frame and a reframe.

When I arrived at this suburban congregation along the Virginia rim of the larger Washington, DC, area, my visionary dreaming joined theirs. The church was seven years of age and saw itself as a progressive, alternative congregation in Southern Baptist circles. I was fresh out of seven years of theological education, eager to "turn on the spigot," the metaphor I remember using. The church and I were fueled by lofty ideals for who we could be and what we could do together. With gusto we engaged the multiple challenges of the day—the pastoral care of congregants serving in Vietnam for a year at a time and their families left behind; the ethical questioning of the war itself; a partner relationship with a strong black Baptist congregation in the center of DC during the Black Power era; unfair housing based on racial differences; and being host church during the Poor People's Campaign. We were dreamers. In Bonhoeffer's words, we "fashioned a visionary ideal of community," both the congregation as community and our geographical area as a just, inclusive community.

In retrospect, that was the *frame*. I was caught up in fulfilling these dreams, these worthy ideals, fueled both by our passion for justice but also our need to be special, different, and better. On that day, sitting on the bench, I saw this frame in the mirror Bonhoeffer lifted before my eyes. To a significant degree I loved the clarity of vision more than I did the people, with all our human ambiguity, immaturity, and flaws. I kept measuring our ministry against these lofty ideals. As Bonhoeffer predicted, I remember times of blaming the church for not meeting these expectations. And, yes, next came the periods of blaming myself for not being enough—strong enough, effective enough—in other words, "a despairing accuser of myself."

The reframe is joining God's love for a particular people in a particular place and time given to us to serve persons as they are. As flawed, imperfect pastors we are given an imperfect congregation to love imperfectly. It's incarnational, not idealistic. We love them and ourselves with all the resources of affirmation, confession, trust, forgiveness, and blessing. This then allows the visioning to be a source of guidance, direction, and inspiration but not the source of judgment.

I took that clarity with me to Pullen, where you joined me as a colleague fifteen years later. That truth from Bonhoeffer didn't eliminate my need and the congregation's need to dream big. The gift in the reframe was self-awareness. I became more likely to see this tendency, thereby giving me a choice of feeding it or not.

In a word, the gift was disillusionment. My illusion or ideal of a special pastor, a special congregation achieving a special vision cracked, then crumbled. It was a costly lesson I needed to learn.

Thanks to you, Dietrich Bonhoeffer.

With gratitude,
Mahan

Notes

[1] Dietrich Bonhoeffer, *Life Together* (New York: Harper & Brothers Publishers, 1954), 27, 28.

[2] Ibid.

Leading within Chronic Anxiety

Dear Nancy,

The content of this letter will not be new to you. I've talked frequently about this practical piece of wisdom. It's an insight I continue to call upon most every day when I'm making sense of human behavior.

Recently, I was visiting with a seasoned pastor who is near retirement. I said, "It's been almost two decades since I helped lead a congregation. All this time you have been at it." Then I asked him, "How is it different now?" His quick response: "There is much more chronic anxiety to deal with!"

I remember precisely when I first heard the phrase "chronic anxiety." In a lecture on leadership, Rabbi Edwin Friedman (referencing his mentor Murray Bowen) said, "Our society is functioning like a *chronically* anxious family."[1] I perked up and took notice. What does that mean? It was such a sweeping comment to make. What I learned changed my pastoral leadership. It became a reframe that mattered.

During my seminary days I learned *about* anxiety. Reinhold Niebuhr wrote about the angst of being human, the inherent anxiety of being finite, feeling uncertain, never in control.[2] Then there was Paul Tillich, who in *The Courage to Be* identified the recurrent human anxieties of fate and death, guilt and condemnation, emptiness and meaninglessness. He believed that the current dominant form of anxiety in our time is meaninglessness.[3] I was also introduced to *acute* anxiety. Much of my pastoral care training was learning skilled, compassionate responses to persons and families in acute crises, the kind of anxiety from loss of life, faith, jobs, health, and relationships.

Of course we *have* anxiety. To be human is to have anxiety. We know regularly this feeling that both constricts and alerts us. I never approached the pulpit without it. I assume the same is true for you.

But *chronic* anxiety is another matter. Here's the difference: Acute anxiety is definable and pinpointed. It results from a specific loss and threat. It has a beginning and ending. In acute anxiety, the loss or threat is keenly experienced, but over time the acuteness in the feeling subsides. The loss of relationship, the loss of a job, the loss of a loved one, the loss of faith, the threat of a pending disaster—all so familiar to pastors—are examples of acute anxiety.

Chronic anxiety, on the other hand, is systemic. It lives within and between us. No clear boundaries. No preciseness. It's in the air we breathe, invisible and potentially explosive like gas fumes in a contained space. All it takes is some critical instant, like striking a match, to ignite an explosion.

Friedman itemized specific behaviors that signal the presence of chronic anxiety, whether expressed in family or workplace or congregation or larger society. I memorized them.

Blaming: the fault is not mine; someone or something else is responsible. By placing the blame elsewhere, a person can avoid any painful acknowledgment of their involvement.

Reactivity: the vicious cycle of intense reactions to events or persons—like billiard balls bouncing off each other. This behavior bypasses the cortex (thoughtful thinking), going directly to the earliest brain, the amygdala (fight, flight, or freeze).

Herding: the polarizing instinct to retreat into camps with each assuming the stance of "us" against "them."

Pushing for a quick fix: the urge to relieve stressful anxiety by pressing for quick solutions.

Does this not mirror our cultural, political, and often religious landscape? We spot this behavior within our primary relationships as well. It feeds distrust, separation, regression, and the lure of fast solutions.[4]

First, let's pause to respect this long-honed capacity for quick reactions. Scientist Brian Swimm grants perspective. It's taken 600,000 years for our nervous systems to develop the capacity to make "sharp local changes" necessary for our survival. Under immediate threat our ancestors had to develop the ability to react swiftly by either fleeing, freezing, or fighting. Now, in our day, the challenge is reversed. In our stage of evolution, Swimm continues, we must learn how to think and plan for long-term possibilities. We must develop our capacity to transcend automatic reactive behavior in the service of collaboration and commitment to long-term solutions.[5]

This understanding of chronic anxiety has everything to do with your work as pastoral leader. You and I have often talked about it. This letter can be a review.

First thing to note: Leadership calls for the opposite of each of these chronically anxious behaviors. When we are leading, in contrast to blaming, we call for assuming responsibility for our participation in both the problem and its resolution. When leading, in contrast to reacting, we call for thoughtful, creative responses. When leading, in contrast to herding or polarizing, we call for collaboration across differences in the pursuit of shared goals. When leading, in contrast to quick fixes, we think with the long term in mind and frame short-term pain as requisite for long-term gain.

No wonder it's so challenging to be a leader in our day! No wonder it often feels like swimming against the tide! No wonder there is a high level of burnout, loneliness, and despair among leaders in all institutions! The climate of chronic anxiety wants to choke the deep breathing required in creative leadership.

Friedman goes on to speculate why there is such a high level of chronic anxiety in our day. The *rapid rate of change* is one. It's the major story of our time. All of us feel, to some degree, overwhelmed by the speed of change. Just consider the pace of technology. It is beyond our ability to absorb its impact, much less to reflect on its meaning. In previous eras change came at an arithmetic pace: 1–2–4–6–8–10–12. Now the pace is exponential: 1–2–4–8–16–32–64.[6]

As an example, at the end of World War II, the full knowledge of human-kind doubled every twenty-five *years*. Today, knowledge doubles every thirteen *months*. Change at this pace keeps our heads spinning from the anxiety of never catching up. It's the state of our daily condition: We need to know more than we can know.

A second source of chronic anxiety is the release of *anxiety binders*. Friedman notes that the anxiety around difference has traditionally been bound in tight, discriminating stereotypes such as racism, anti-Semitism, sexism, classism, and heterosexism.[7] While we celebrate the cracking open of these binding prejudices, we are also left with the additional anxiety of uncertainty. Before, relationships were defined with clear boundaries. Now, in relationships of diversity, we find ourselves in unfamiliar, uncharted territory. We fear saying the wrong word or doing the wrong act. We are dancing with no clear steps in place. For most of us, the commitment is clear: to keep risking relationships on multiple fronts across differences.

Assuming that we lead from within an atmosphere of chronic anxiety, how then do we practice leadership? In two ways this understanding has gifted me as pastor. One is *external*. The other is *internal*.

When I notice the outward chronic anxiety in play (in myself or others)—through blaming, polarizing, reactivity, or pushes for quick fixes—I know to stop and take notice. To push ahead is futile. At that point I know not to expect much learning or creative problem-solving to happen. I know that denying this behavior won't be helpful. I'm aware that overpowering the anxiety will only fuel the flames. This leaves us the immediate task to look for ways to reduce the anxiety both in the situation and in myself.

Our own responses can often turn down the wick of collective anxiety. These developed skills might include listening fully and reflecting your understanding to the satisfaction of the other(s) before you respond with your ideas. Sometimes it helps to call into the conversation the purpose for coming together. This reminder of common values and commitment may soften the polarities. One leader I've experienced, when in the midst of reactive discussions, calls for a few minutes of silence. Other leaders are adept in using humor to defuse the anxiety. Such responses encourage the lowering of chronic anxiety so that the creativity within mutuality can return.

The other response is *internal*, going inside even in the midst of chronic anxiety. Sometimes the only thing you can do is to exercise the only control you have—that is, working with your own anxiety. You have the capacity, if developed, to refrain from reactive blaming or polarizing behavior. A low-anxious presence is a response you can offer. This does not mean you are not anxious. It means you find ways to reduce your own anxiety so you can be less anxious within your role as leader.

Offering a non-anxious presence may not seem productive. It looks that way. Indeed, its power cannot be easily measured and is easily underestimated. But just call to mind a crisis in the church or nation or family. When crises occur, the eyes of everyone turn to the leader. We look for the leader's responses. Those in the position of leadership are like thermostats. If they exude calmness, confidence, and no anxiety (regardless of what they are feeling inside), their presence will lower the heat (anxiety). The opposite is also true. An anxious leader will elevate the anxiety for everyone. It's the nature of all systems. In times of crises, we take our emotional cues from leaders. Anxiety is contagious. So is a calm presence.

You and I have access to another resource. You are not just a leader whose non-anxious presence invites a lowering of systemic anxiety. As noted in a former reframe, you are a living symbol of More Than You Are. Your presence, for some, points to a larger Presence. In experiencing you, they may experience what you represent to them—the presence of a community, the presence of trust, the presence of God.

You have your own ways of lowering your inner anxiety and maximizing outward presence. Know them, use them, and expand your repertoire. Fortunately, we live in a time when there is a plethora of technologies that foster centered non-anxiousness in the midst of chronic anxiety. To notice when and how you are being triggered into reactive behavior is a key discipline to master. This awareness from stepping back and inner observing grants options in responding. It is lifelong interior work that I will address more fully in a later letter on contemplative practicing.

You have heard me reference Martin Laird's metaphor, my favorite shorthand for this practice: "I am the mountain, not the weather."[8] Your identity and mine, the grace of Being, being loved and loving, if we allow it, can be our center, our identity as solid as a mountain. All else, the array of reactive thoughts and feelings, come and go like the weather. The weather will change and pass, but not the mountain. You are the mountain, not the weather.

This understanding of chronic anxiety from Edwin Friedman opened my eyes to the anxious driven behaviors swirling around us. It gave me names. It uncovered the source of these behaviors. It invited me to notice the difference between reacting and responding. And from this reframe I could see where to focus my energy, not so much on the behaviors, but on the anxiety at their base.

I was left with a question that I now leave with you: How can I be a pastoral leader *within* chronic anxiety but not *of* it?

With gratitude,
Mahan

Notes

[1] Friedman, *A Failure of Nerve*, 58–93.

[2] In *Nature and Destiny of Man* Reinhold Niebuhr writes about this human angst, our original state of sin. As humans we keep conceiving and desiring perfection while being incapable of achieving it.

[3] In *Courage to Be* Tillich interprets anxiety as being the threat of non-being. Courage is the self-affirmation of one's being in spite of the threat of non-being.

[4] Friedman explores these behavioral expressions of living within chronic anxiety in Chapter Two, "A Society in Regression," *A Failure of Nerve*, 51–94.

[5] I learned this distinction from Brian Swimme, teacher of evolutionary cosmology from his documentary "Journey of the Universe."

[6] This reference to the exponential, rapid pace of life as one source of contemporary chronic anxiety I heard in a series of Friedman lectures. This reference along with the following allusion to "anxiety binders" does not appear in *The Failure of Nerve*, a book published from his lectures after his sudden death on October 31, 1996.

[7] Ibid.

[8] Martin Laird, *Into the Silent Land* (Oxford: University Press, 2006), 86.

Triangling in the Text

Dear Nancy,

This could be two letters, but I'm staying with one since the two different contexts are held together by one piece of theory from family systems—the triangle.

Murray Bowen observed that life insists on homeostasis—that is, balance and stability. For example, a tripod requires three legs, not two, in order to be stable. Or when one part of a mobile is changed, the whole mobile is thrown out of balance until a new balance is regained. That movement toward balance and stability is nature's way, including human nature.

When two human beings feel unstable, they will often "triangle" in a third person or third issue as a way to reduce the tension between them, hence recovering the balance being threatened with instability. You know the experience. Think of two parishioners in conflict who "triangle" you in as the problem-solver. Or you may be triangled as *the* problem. Either way, the stress of imbalance is reduced in their relationship while leaving you holding the anxiety. Or imagine that you and a friend, perhaps a spouse, are engaging in a conversation that is taking you both out of your comfort zone. One of you "triangles" in some other issue or some other person in the conversation, like your child's behavior, in order to reduce the discomfort and reinstate the stability. This way of maintaining balance and avoiding change in relationships is frequent and largely unconscious.

Now let's look at preaching. In Walter Brueggemann's article "The Preacher, the Text, and the People," he lifts from Murray Bowen this idea of *triangle* and uses it in a positive way.[1]

First, he describes the typical understanding of preaching that sees the sermon happening between pastor/preacher (A) and people/congregation (B). It sure looks that way. The preacher in the pulpit addressing people in the pews. Preacher speaking, congregation listening. Preacher interpreting Scripture with the people responding internally. That's the way it seems, preaching as the interaction between preacher (A) and congregation (B). If so, the focus is on the performance of the preacher. Congregants will like or dislike what they hear, probably a combination of both. Over the Sunday dinner conversation might be the questions: How do you think she did today? Or how was his sermon for you?

Brueggemann draws from Bowen's family system's theory to bring forward a positive use of "triangle." What if, he suggests, the voice of the biblical text is "triangled" in as "C"?

(C) text

preacher (A)   (B) congregation

He is not suggesting a "tipping of the hat" to the text. Rather, in Brueggemann's thinking, the preacher must be tethered to the text. The text, not the preacher, is the focus. You as the preacher (A), along with the congregation (B), both come under the authority of the text (C). It's the text that matters.

I'm quite sure, Nancy, that we have talked about this insight from Brueggemann, for his reframe changed my understanding of preaching. When I read it, I remember feeling relief. My job was no longer to make something happen. My job was to engage the meaning of the text *out loud*, hoping the sermon would stimulate members to do the same—that is, to engage the text as their experience. From that stance I became more prompter than expert, more inquisitive than indisputable, more challenging than dogmatic, more playful than certain. I came to relish the freedom to explore, fuss, imagine, interpret the text visibly in public, praying that my words might provoke a substantive engagement between listener and text, "B" with "C," parishioner with Spirit. As preacher I was saying in effect, "Friends, this is what I see, feel, and hear in this text. Here is where it takes me. This is where it can take us. Where does it take you? Where do you sense this text taking us as a congregation?" This became a huge reframing for me.

James Lamkin, in a companion article in the same periodical that includes Brueggemann's words, describes his role as preacher in this triangle: "The preacher is present to what is happening between God and the listener, *but the preacher is not responsible for that relationship*. Occasionally, I will say something like, 'I, as a preacher, don't know what to make of this difficult text, either. But it is *my* job to remind *you* that it is in *our* Bibles. *Each of us* is responsible for *our* response to *God*.'"[2]

This perspective I found to be profoundly liberating. When I allowed it, it minimized the performance quotient in preaching. No longer did I feel at the center of the action. I was free, even if only partially, from the arrogant illusion to change people through my words. The attempt to interpret brilliantly, craft eloquently, and deliver a sermon to be remembered was never totally absent. This new stance did help me push these ego voices to the background, where their noise was softer. In my better moments I could feel the thrill and privilege of engaging the text in preparation and then in public, allowing the Spirit within the text to do her work on all of us. Brueggemann changed my understanding of preaching, and to the degree I allowed it, he changed my practice of preaching.

I offer another insight from "triangling," also a positive use of this theory. This example of triangling in the text can illumine our leadership as well as our preaching.

Every congregation I know has a purpose (mission) statement. Functionally, we can say it's the congregation's text to be heard, studied, and followed. The good ones are crisp and short.

In my early years at Pullen, before you came in 1992, I felt that we too needed a purpose statement that emerged from a congregational process. But it never found any feet, much less traction. One night it dawned on our little committee that we already had a purpose statement. We had one and hadn't named it as such. I'm told that my predecessors, both Finlator and Poteat, preached regularly on Micah 6:8. Maybe it was annually. This verse has been central to me as well. And I heard it referenced occasionally in conversations around the church. We were trying to create a purpose that had emerged organically: "What does the LORD require of you? To do justice, love mercy, walk humbly with God" (Micah 6:8). All we had to do was name what had been implicit. From what I gather, under your leadership this Bible verse still continues to be the text you keep triangling into the church's life together.

In my experience, purpose or mission statements seldom stay alive and active in congregational life. They are displayed somewhere on a wall and website or worship bulletin or may be hidden away in a file labeled "Important Documents." Rarely are they listened to for inspiration and guidance in decision-making, program-making, service-making, vision-making, and especially leadership-making. Amnesia sets in.

Frederic Laloux, in his book *Reinventing Organizations*, gives evidence for the crucial importance of repeatedly "triangling" in such purpose statements and Purpose more broadly. Laloux's research is built on the assumption that institutions in our time of accelerating change are being pressed to reinvent themselves. He studied global organizations that navigated successfully a process of reinventing themselves. He particularly focused on the leadership required in these reinventions. The leaders shared these qualities:

- They focus on the clear, compelling Purpose of the organization while at the same time experimenting freely with structures or programs.
- They hire colleagues equally excited about the Purpose.
- In contrast to a precise future vision, they trust that new forms, directions, programs will emerge from regularly listening to the "text," their Purpose.
- They place Purpose over profit or survival.

Laloux notes one practice that I found particularly intriguing. One executive, when meeting with his leadership council, would place an *empty chair* at the table to represent the Purpose of the organization. During the discussion of organizational matters, anyone on the council at any time could move from their chair to the *empty chair* and speak to the decision-making discussion from the perspective of the Purpose. They might say, "This is how I see or don't see our discussion aligning with our Purpose."[3]

I think if I were pastor again, I would experiment in a committee meeting with an actual, physical empty chair representing the viewpoint of Purpose (our congregational Text). But more to the point, I would be more intentional about finding multiple ways to keep before the church our Purpose/Text, the "Why are we here?"

Purpose or mission speaks to motivation, the deepest motivation. It challenges us to consider our reasons for belonging to a congregation. There are many reasons: the preaching or liturgy or architecture or programs. A mixture, no doubt, and mostly unconscious. But only Purpose calls us collectively to a vision and hope larger than ourselves. It's sustaining, never runs out, has no end, becoming the tread to follow from generation to generation.

Most everyone I read these days assumes that the church is experiencing a major transition, perhaps as great as the Reformation 500 years ago. If so, along with other major institutions, most congregations are in the business of reinventing themselves. This "paradigm" shift, as it is sometimes named, is true today in a way it was not when I began my ministry during post-WWII years. In those days, our Purpose was to *grow*; our message was *come*. Now, numerical growth is less likely. Members are reexamining their beliefs. Congregations are reviewing their programs, structure, and worship styles.

Perhaps in our day we are being driven wonderfully and painfully back to the essentials: Who are we as a congregation? Why are we here? What are we for? What is our calling? What does it mean as a community to incarnate the justice-love of God in our time and place? What primary Text are we understanding, standing under?

"There is nothing so practical as a good theory," I remember hearing in some distant conference. I find it true. This piece of family systems theory—the triangle—is a good example. It opened up for me two applications: triangling in the Text in preaching and triangling in Purpose as our Text in leadership.

With gratitude,
Mahan

Notes

[1] Walter Brueggemann, "The Preacher, the Text and the People," (*Theology Today*, 47, 1990), 237–247.

[2] James Lampkin, "Systems Theory and Congregational Leadership," (*Review and Expositor*, 102, summer 2005), 471.

[3] Frederic Lalouz, *Reinventing Organizations* (Brussels, Belgium: Nelson Parker, 2014). Frederic Lalouz in his research of organizations re-inventing themselves does not include congregations. But I found this book profoundly relevant to pastoral leadership. If it's true, along with every major institution, churches are having to reinvent themselves amid irrelevance and appeals for change, then this book is for church leaders as well. The "empty chair" in the middle of the circle of decision makers—representing Purpose—underscores the critical voice of Purpose in organizations experiencing transition.

Engaging Death as Practice

Dear Nancy,

I have saved what seems particularly unique to our vocation for this last letter in this section. I don't see this topic named in literature or hear it in "shop talk" among pastors. Maybe the intimate nature of it makes it so.

Let's allow the word *practice* to convey its double meaning: a *profession*, as in the practice of medicine or psychotherapy; and *practicing* for learning, as in piano practice or spiritual practice. In both ways pastors engage death as a practice.

We begin with the first meaning—pastor in a *practice that specializes*. If, let's say, Alisa as an attorney practices law and Alan as a therapist practices psychotherapy, then Ava as a pastor practices death and dying. Death and dying are her specialty. Death and dying is your specialty. Death and dying was my specialty.

Nancy, I can hear the quick rebuttal: "But I have heard you say often what I have heard from a host of others that pastoral ministry is one of the last generalist professions." Indeed, I have said that often. And I think it's true. We are general practitioners. We are expected to have competence in diverse, multiple roles: preaching, teaching, designing, and directing worshipful rituals; leading and managing an institution; caring and counseling individual and families; writing and speaking; and offering a responsible presence in the wider church and community.

So I'll modify my statement: You are a general practitioner with a specialty. That specialty is engaging death. For you and other pastors, the presence of death is always close by. If the shaman Don Juan counsels Carlos Castaneda to heed death's wisdom as a companion just over his left shoulder, then for pastors the presence of death is in front of our nose. Most people can keep at bay the reality of death, denying its inevitability as out of sight, out of mind. Not so with pastors. Not so with you.

For you, death is ever present. While you scamper from appointment to appointment, there is on the edge of your consciousness always a member experiencing some kind of profound death—the loss of a loved one, job, health, marriage, home, hope, status, memory, or perhaps a worldview crumbling from the weight of irrelevance. You carry this concern moving in and out of your awareness. Death stalks the halls of hospitals you regularly visit. In nursing homes you see its presence in the gaunt, vacant eyes you pass by and whose faces light up with the slightest attention. You frequent homes experiencing the raw grief of some wrenching loss. You hear loss in memories shared, in the photographs exchanged, and in "groans too deep for words." In every service of worship, whether funerals, weddings, or regular weekly gatherings, some members are always present with moistened eyes, feeling the pain of a particular loss welling up from deep within. The privacy of a church sanctuary within a safe community can provide the sacred space for felt grief to surface. In all directions death is close, ever near.

Consider your role in the dying and death of a parishioner: present during the phase of dying, whether extended or short term; present during the days around the death, including the preparation and leadership of corporate rituals; and present during the aftercare of continued grieving. Other professionals—physicians, nurses, chaplains, funeral directors, lawyers, financial planners, therapists—have their unique roles, but the pastor is, or can be, the point of continuity, a possible overseer of this sometimes lengthy process.

Pastors, depending on the constituency of the congregation they serve, will have many or few deaths of members in a given year. In my first congregation, a church of young families, I led about two or three funerals a year. In my last congregation with you at Pullen, we had as many as twelve or more funerals each year.

But regardless of the number of funerals, the death and dying experience far exceeds the physical deaths. Grieving is so much larger. Loss is experienced in multiple forms. We could even say that most of pastoral care is grief work in one way or another. Death and dying, in its various expressions, is our specialty. It's our forte.

This part of our work is not an option. Other aspects of our ministry may be slighted but not this one. This practice must be done with effectiveness. It must be. Like no other pastoral function, the skilled care offered around losses will either *deepen* or *distance* the relationship between you and the people under your care. You know this truth: Faithfulness in this specialty is not forgotten; unfaithfulness in this specialty is also not forgotten and likely not forgiven. As I see it, your faithfulness in this ministry is a major reason why you are passing the quarter-century mark as a minister at Pullen. I cannot even imagine the number of funerals or memorial services you have led during your service to this congregation. No one told me the crucial importance of this ministry during seminary years, or if they did, I wasn't listening. I learned it on the run, on the job, realizing early that this priority mattered.

My doctor has his practice. My lawyer has her practice. When you engage the dying and death of any significant loss, then that's your practice. It's a specialty.

The second dimension to this reframe is more personal. As I turned into my mid-fifties, entering my last decade as pastor, I remember a clarity that came into focus. My death is not too far away. Now living in the "December" of my life, it's clearer still. I'm raising with you the following question: What if our being so near to dying and death became a personal spiritual practice, "a fringe benefit" of our work?

Cloistered monks, I'm told, will whisper occasionally to each other, "*Memento mori*" (remember death). Don't you hear that whisper? From walking through the corridors of a nursing home lined with patients humped over, medicated to a vacant stare, you hear the whisper: "Remember death." In the car driving away from the bedside of a member dying, there is the same whisper in your ears: "Remember death." In the funeral home and at the graveside, there is the whisper again: "Remember death. You too will die. So will your loved ones. So will your friends. So will your vocation. It's only a matter of time." And even standing by a crib of a newborn, perhaps your child or grandchild, while marveling over the mysterious gift of life, you experience their fragile, vulnerable existence. You feel the edge of limits. This new person will live for a time, then pass. Even there, you hear that whisper.

Some might cry in response, "Morbid!" But you know its truth. You understand the paradox that in facing death, life becomes more vivid and precious. Limits highlight what's within them. Every experience of dying and death, with any awareness on our part, will peel back the layers to the core clarity of what matters, what really matters.

I'm just reminding you of what you know from experience. When I was with someone dying and who was sufficiently conscious of that fact, I remember thinking that the scene seemed like the last judgment. Either they die into feeling loving and being loved or they feel the profound pain of its absence. It's holy ground. The veil is pulled back to reveal the truth of what is. There is an unspoken question in the room: "Did I live well?" or "Did I love well?" or "Did we love you well?" There's no wiggle room. No ambiguity. It's yes or no.

If Love is the shining truth at death, either by its presence or absence, why can it not be the shining truth in our living? Why wait? In advance we can begin to let go of attachments that compete with our core identity as Love. Why not, in the words of Friar David Steindl-Rast, "learn to let go of so much along the way that death becomes only a step away from God"?[1] In her book *Love Stronger Than Death*, Cynthia Bourgeault adds that the "after life" begins not when our body dies but when this gesture of surrender [to Love] is mastered. And I'm fond of her dying friend Rafe's challenge: "You have to find that part of you [Love] that already is beyond death and start to live out of that *now*."[2]

I'm saying that pastors have a better chance than most. We, because of our vocation, have more opportunities to discover in our near-death experiences the occasions for spiritual practice. Our very work reminds us of what lasts and doesn't last, what matters and what doesn't. We get to practice what we on occasion offer the dying in those last moments: "It's okay to release your grip. You can trust the Love around you and the Love that receives you."

Truth be told, the beauty of this spiritual practice is now for me more timely. When we were pastors together, even in my last years, my death seemed decades away. Now, at eighty-four, this whisper of "remember death" is amplified. The volume is up. And I am listening.

This letter, the last part, may not feel imperative or even pertinent to you. If so, let it be an anchor to throw well into your future. Then, in the future, as your mortality becomes more a felt reality, you might want to pull on this anchor occasionally as a way forward in your spiritual work of letting go. Consider the possibility that engaging so much death, as you do, gives you a head start. Try it on as a spiritual practice.

In this letter I have challenged your imagination with two reframes. Both might feel unusual. You are more than a generalist. You also have a professional practice, a specialty in relating to the dying and death of congregants. You are a generalist with a specialty.

Second, I am considering with you another understanding of practice. Your frequent near-death experiences that come with the job just might be a form of spiritual practice. The poet Rumi calls this "dying before you die."[3] Jesus calls this "losing or dying to your life to find it" (Luke 17:33). The apostle Paul calls it "dying to rise into newness of life" (Romans 6:4). Benedict calls it "keeping death daily before your eyes (*memento mori*)."[4]

Nancy, before I conclude this letter, I want to register my slight discomfort. I stand by the points I am making, but seeing ourselves as professionals must remain a soft, secondary identity. In my seminary days, the master of divinity degree was promoted as a professional degree on the level of a master's degree in social work. That emphasis felt to me even then as an effort to achieve equal secular status. It seemed to come from a sense of inferiority. Frankly, I prefer the title of amateur. *Amateur* means lover, ones who love what they are doing. When visiting the hospitals, for instance, I proudly felt like an amateur, representing the world of love and community within a world of professional specialists. So while I still value our work as a practice with a specialty, at its heart we are not specialists, but amateurs who participate in divine love.

Appropriately this letter on death ends this second section of the book. The third section I regard to be foundational to them all.

With gratitude,
Mahan

Notes

[1] See Kenneth Kramer, "Dying Before Dying," an interview with Brother David Stendl-Rast, *Journal of Ecumenical Studies*, 2010.

[2] Bourgeault, Cynthia, *Love Is Stronger Than Death* (New York: Praxis Publishing, 2007), 221.

[3] This phrasing is attributed to Sufi poet Mathnewe Rumi. See *Mathnewe Rumi*, vol. I: pp. 754–758 by Carry We and Kabir Helmiske (Threshold Books, 1995).

[4] "Memento mori," Latin for "remember your death," long associated with St. Benedict's Rule, exhorts monks to "keep death daily."

Section III

Formation and Transformation

Dear Nancy,

I have positioned these last three letters in a separate section. They are about personal transformation. I know that for you and many others transformation is at the heart of your life, but I don't want to assume that all pastors see it this way, nor do I want to judge those for whom it is not. There are many ministers who are well-formed, fully equipped pastors who offer effective ministry.

I think the philosopher-mystic Ken Wilber got it right. Religion—Christianity in our case—performs two important but different functions. Most people turn to the church for strengthening their individual, separate lives. They seek a counternarrative to their life being merely "a tale told by an idiot, full of sound and fury, signifying nothing."[1] Parishioners seek meaning. They want their batteries charged. Members of our congregations expect from a service of worship the sustenance to face another week with hope. We understand and appreciate this function. You and I work for this good outcome.

A minority of persons, according to Wilber, want radical transformation, a transcending while including the individual separate self.[2] What dies is our efforts for well-being through personal striving. Maybe that's the way transformation works. Our efforts to prove and earn and achieve and think correctly have to break down along the way—break down and break us open. What's transcended is the assumption that being separate individuals is all that we are. It seems that many, even most, people know nothing other than their ego consciousness, their personality, and the personalities of others.

Nancy, we are thinking together about the second function of religion—transformation. I'm raising with you the key possibility of our lives: the movement from our primary identity as separate self (small self) to our essential identity as beloved of God—being loved and loving justly. *Trans*, means "more, going beyond." We are moving beyond our small and separate self to our core identity as "rooted and grounded" in divine love. In this letter we are looking at this dance, this back and forth journey from formation to transformation, from I, but not I, Christ living in and through me (paraphrase Gal 2:20).

Just as it should be, you and I attended the seminary to be *formed* as individual pastors. Multiple resources comprise this preparation: understanding church history; tools for interpreting Scripture and culture; analytical thinking; self-understanding; exposure to leading worship and congregational life; and pastoral skills in caring, particularly in times of personal, familial, and congregational crises.

For some of us there comes a time when being well-formed is insufficient. Cracks appear in our formed container. Sometimes these cracks in our formation come early in our ministry, sometimes later, sometimes not at all.

This crack in my formation appeared during my first full-time leadership of a congregation. I entered this work with the excitement of feeling fully formed by years of university and seminary preparation. From the beginning, my work felt purposeful, full of meaning. Most mornings I would rise from my bed anticipating the day. As I reflect back on this time, I realize I was experiencing what the Franciscan Richard Rohr (with depth psychologist Carl Jung whispering in his ears) calls completing the work of the "first half of life."[3] I felt established in the role. I was confident. That worked well—until it didn't.

As referenced in a few other letters, the cracks became deeper. It was a turbulent, anxious time, 1967–1972, particularly within the DC area: the height of the Vietnam War (about half of our congregation were military families), assassinations (Martin Luther King Jr., Robert Kennedy), the Poor People's Campaign. In those days I'm sure I preached and taught personal transformation. No doubt I declared the grace of God as gift and not our achievement. But functionally I felt this work was up to me, and after about five years my "me" was not up to the challenge. Pastoral work began to exhaust the love that gave birth to it. With deepening personal dismay, plus our young family of six needing more of me, I resigned. I left the congregation. I left the role. Gratefully, I landed with a good ministry in a hospital setting that gave me the space and community to process the meaning of my decision. Years later I felt ready and eager to return to the challenge of congregational leadership. Pullen gave me that opportunity, one that I enjoyed for fifteen years until retirement. The return felt like a second marriage, a second attempt, a new chance to be what I most loved—a pastor.

During those transition years a reframe began to emerge with force. There must be more. With focused intention—actually more like an insatiable longing—I began to explore what Ken Wilber describes as radical transformation, the transcending the ego-centeredness of the separate self.[4]

This thread was there all along in those familiar passages we know so well. From Jesus: lose your life to find it; take up your cross and follow (Luke 17:33; Matt 16:25); a grain of wheat falling into the ground, dying, husks broken open, yielding a rich harvest (John 12:24); not my will but Thine be done (Mark 14:36); love as I have loved you (John 13:34). you must be born from above… of Spirit (John 3: 3–8).

And from Paul the same themes of transformation: in baptism a dying to rise in newness of life (Rom 5:3–4); I live now, not I, the Christ-life lives in me (Gal 2:20); being transformed by degrees into the likeness of Christ (2 Cor 3:18); being transforming by the renewing of your minds, so that you may discern what is the will of God (Rom 12: 2); taking on the mind or consciousness of Christ as kenosis, a self-emptying, non-clinging, self-giving love no matter the cost (Phil 2:4–11).

Perhaps a clever parable can scrape away the glaze from these overly familiar passages and reveal just how breathtaking this change really is. This parable devised by Maurice Nicoll in the 1950s has been revised by Jacob Needleman, then by Cynthia Bourgeault in *The Wisdom Way of Knowing*, and now slightly by me:

> Once upon a time, in a not-so-faraway land, there was a kingdom of acorns, nestled at the foot of a grand old oak tree. Since the citizens of his kingdom were modern, fully Westernized acorns, there were spas for oiling and polishing those shells and various acornopathic therapies to enhance longevity and well-being. They went about their business with purposeful energy. They were busy developing their human potential, taking advantage of books and conferences that enhanced self-actualization. There were seminars called "Getting All You Can Out of Your Shell." There were woundedness and recovery groups for acorns who had been bruised in their original fall from the tree.
>
> One day, in the midst of this kingdom, there suddenly appeared a knotty little stranger, apparently dropped "out of the sky" by a passing bird. He was capless and dirty, making an immediate negative impression on his fellow acorns. And crouched beneath the oak tree, he stammered out a wild tale. Pointing upward toward the tree, he said, "We…are…that!"
>
> Delusional thinking, obviously, the other acorns concluded, but one of them continued to engage him in conversation: "So tell us, how would we become that tree?"
>
> "Well," said he, "pointing downward, "it has something to do with going into the ground…and cracking open the shell."

"Insane," they responded. "Totally morbid! Why, then we wouldn't be acorns anymore."

This we know about acorns: they are seeds. It is their nature and destiny to become oak trees. Acorns, to be true to what they are, must fall into the ground and die as acorns, allowing their shells to be cracked open, all the while taking into themselves the nourishment of soil, water, and sun. Acorns are made to yield to a force greater than themselves. In time they become oak trees.

Let's place this parable alongside Jesus's similar metaphor: "Unless a grain of wheat falls into the ground and dies, it remains just a single grain, but if it dies, it shall yield a rich harvest" (John 12:24).

Could this be true? Are we more than merely biological accidents in a world of random events? Are we even more than well-formed, reasonably healthy individuals? Are we made for a transformation as amazing as the acorn becoming an oak tree or a grain becoming wheat or losing oneself for a fuller, more authentic one? Is that magnificent possibility coiled within us? Is there an identity in us that is beyond a strong, polished personality (acorn)? The gospel narrative says "yes," a resounding "yes!"

My "yes" was weak but strengthening. Before returning to being pastor, this possibility became my primary curiosity and hope.

The focus on identity was where this mystery of inner transformation landed within me. Identity is where we locate ourselves. Beloved is one name for this new identity. Other names include child of God, Christ-consciousness, Christ-likeness, Christ-ness, Christ living in us, True Self, or image of God. Thomas Merton puts it concisely: "To say we are made in the image of God is to say that love is the reason for my existence, for God is love. Love is my true identity. Selflessness is my true self. Love is my true character. Love is my name."[5]

Is this radical transformation the transfer to a deeper identity? If so, "Mahan" and "Nancy" are secondary identities—significant and unique but secondary. Our primary identity is Love—God's love. We experience this Love as a verb, not a noun. It's a verb, and it's relational. It's a constant receiving and giving, a self-filling and self-giving, like breathing in, breathing out. This shift in identity is variously named: from self to Self, from ego-centered to God-centered, from false self to True Self, from individual self to interbeing, from separate self (Mahan and Nancy) to Love as our name and being.

The trapeze artist, I'm told, must not *try* to be caught. That's when accidents happen. Instead, they must allow themselves to be caught. That's the hard part for me. During the early years, I tried hard to make ministry happen. There's a place for hard work. But inner transformation calls for letting go, surrender, allowing ourselves to be caught.

In the words of my banjo teacher, responding to my question about her performance anxiety, "When I can get to the place within myself and with others when the Music is more important than I am, then I am not anxious." That's it. That's the sense of transformation: To so identify with the Music that we become relatively free of self-consciousness.

But the Music doesn't happen without the banjo and banjo player. That is, in transformation we do not eliminate the egoic self, as if that's desirable or even possible. In fact, it takes a strong ego, a well-formed ego, to do the work of ministry. You are a "sitting duck," out in the open, vulnerable to the spoken and unspoken demands, criticisms, and expectations coming toward you. Most of the time there is little you can do to defend yourself. Required is a solid sense of self.

But I came to see that being a mature personality is not all that we are. You and I are more. The ego, our personality, is transcended and included. Like an electrical plug, by itself it's incomplete. It is designed to be plugged into electrical currents. The untruth is seeing ourselves as separate. The plug and electrical current need each other.

Jesus said as much. You are like a branch, unique and distinct but useless for fruit-bearing if not connected to the vine. Transformation is about being connected to the Source of energy. The ego, like a separate branch on the vine, maintains its value but disowns its claim as primary identity.

I realize, Nancy, that I am bombarding you with metaphors. In this letter we are immersing ourselves in a Mystery of inner transformation that, while ineffable, yet demands our efforts at speech, stories, and metaphors. I have noted a few, mostly from Jesus. I will add two that stay alive in me.

Krista Tippett, in an interview with the civil rights leader Congressman John Lewis about the "bloody Sunday" event in Selma, Alabama, in 1965, asked, "When you were protesting on the Edmund Pettus Bridge and facing the fury of the police coming at you with billy clubs threatening your very life, how could you love then? How could you love them?" Lewis responded, "Oh, but you need to understand. *The love is already there. I just join it.*"[6]

Lewis names this Mystery. Love is not something we generate within us and then give away. We don't "try" to love. Love cannot be willed. The force of Love, as Lewis is saying, is already present as a power we join. It's a magnetic energy field to which we relate, in which we participate, and to which we add. This realm of God, as Jesus declared, is within and between us, a relational matrix of grace "in whom we live and move and have our being" (Acts 17:28). Some awaken to this Reality; some do not. Some join this Love; some do not. Some surrender to its energy; others do not. To be transformed is to yield to and align with this Power and be carried by its currents.

"Being carried by its currents" comes from Rainer Rilke in his poem "The Swan." It's another metaphor of this shift from ego or small self to deeper Self. Rilke pictures the awkwardness of a swan out of water on its own, "lumbering as if in ropes through what is not done." The transformation occurs when the swan lets go of his feet on the ground, "nervously lets himself down into the water… which flows joyfully under and after him, wave after wave…marvelously calm… *pleased to be carried.*"[7]

That's the movement: from the awkwardness of daily lumbering with the ego's great effort to complete "what is not done" to letting ourselves down into the currents of Love that joyfully carry us forward. Call it "losing your life to find it" or "not my will but thine be done" or "not I but Christ living in me" or "kenosis, the non-clinging self-emptying." All these phrases express the transforming motion of yielding to and allowing ourselves to be carried by currents of divine love.

The swan makes it look easy. So does John Lewis. But we know it's not. The challenge can be expressed as working with the tension of two identities. A friend, Dan Synder, expresses these two identities in this way: I am by grace a *child of God*; I am by birth a *child of Pharaoh*. I am both. You are both.

When many decades ago I read these words from William Sloan Coffin— "I'm Pharaoh to everybody's liberation movement"[8]—I said, "yes, me too." His words were a mirror. I'm a child of Pharaoh born into privilege: white, male, heterosexual, middle upper class, advanced education, American. I was born into domination systems, to use Walter Wink's phrase. I was born on third base. You were born on second base. We are children of Pharaoh.

You and I are working with acknowledging our privilege, confessing it, realizing its power, and choosing over and over again to act from and for relationships of equity, justice, and partnership. That's our summons. It's painful, unending work trying to let go of patterns centuries in the making. We take minuscule steps toward that inner freedom. My hope? That our incremental steps will be picked up and advanced by our children and grandchildren and great-grandchildren.

I'm suggesting that within this dismantling we are given a place to stand. We are given a secure identity from which to risk this soul work. By being solidly grounded in our primary identity as grace, as unconditionally loved, we find the energy and courage to steward our privilege, using its power for justice and disconnecting from its power to dominate. This is inner soul work: finding energy from being a child of God to face the implications of being a child of Pharaoh.

I'll end this letter with some homemade affirmations I sometimes repeat. They give me a feel for this movement between formation and transformation.

> I have a ministry, but I am not primarily my ministry. At the core, my identity is Love, beloved, being loved, and loving justly.
>
> I have a separate, unique personality, but I am not primarily my personality. At the core, my name is Love, beloved, being loved, and loving justly.
>
> I have successes and failures, but I am not primarily either. At the core, my name is Love, beloved, being loved, and loving justly.
>
> I am a child of Pharaoh born into privileges of power not earned, powers that more wound than liberate, but I am not primarily my privileges. At the core, my name is Love, beloved, being loved, and loving justly.[9]

The following last two letters are sequels to this one. The three belong together. This letter is for insight, a "seeing into" the dynamics of transformation. But we know that insight by itself is not transformative. Changes require practice. The next letter focuses on transformative practices. The final letter proposes that your ministry itself can be a spiritual practice of inner transformation.

With gratitude,
Mahan

Postscript

We have been thinking about transformation. Merton, in *The Reflections of a Guilty Bystander*, reached deep within for words that capture both the content and particularly the feel of this intimate experience:

In Louisville, at the corner of Fourth and Walnut, in the center of the shopping district, I was suddenly overwhelmed with the realization that I loved all these people, that they were mine and I theirs…. that we could not be alien to one another even though we were total strangers. It was like *waking from a dream of separateness*, of spurious self. But it cannot be explained. There is no way of telling people that they are all walking around shining like the sun…. If only they could see themselves as they are. If only we could see each other that way all the time.[10]

Notes

[1] William Shakespeare, *Macbeth*, Act 5, scene 5.

[2] Ken Wilbur, *The Essential Ken Wilbur* (Boston, MA: Shambhala Publications, 1998), 140–143.

[3] Richard Rohr, *Falling Upward* (Francisco, CA: Jossey-Bass, 2011).
In this book, drawing on C.C Jung's "two halves of life," Rohr describes the breakdown of the "first half" that may open to the "second half of life" where the soul transcends ego as central identity.

[4] Wilbur, *The Essential Ken Wilbur*, 141.

[5] Thomas Merton, *Seeds of Contemplation* (New York: Dell Publishing Co., 1949), 23.

[6] From Krista Tippet's interview with Congressman and civil rights leader, John Lewis, *On Being*, January 26, 2017.

[7] In the poem "The Swan" Rainer Maria Rilke (1875–1926) compares the awkward waddling of a swan to the awkwardness of daily living from one commitment to another. The contrast is the swan letting herself down into the water, yielding gracefully to being carried by its currents.

[8] William Sloan Coffin named this awareness—"I am Pharaoh to everyone's liberation movement—either in a book of sermons or a taped sermon from Riverside Church. I am unable to trace its precise origin. I immediately identified with his self-awareness. In my lifetime, while I have, in some measure, participated in the multiple movements of liberation, nevertheless, as one born into privilege, I have reeled from their confrontations and calls for transformation. I am a child of Pharaoh.

[9] While the content is mine, the frame of "I have a [ministry], but I am not my [ministry]" is from Ken Wilbur, *No Boundary* (Boston: Shambhala, 1979), 114, 115.

[10] Thomas Merton, *Reflections of a Guilty Bystander* (New York: Doubleday, 196), 156–158.

Transformative Practice

Dear Nancy,

You know me well. You know my love of insights. To read or hear something that pulls back the veil on a new understanding is thrilling for me. I may be addicted. I love the adrenaline rush of a new "aha!"

But insight by itself is not transformative—much to my chagrin. I love ideas. While thinking, teaching, and preaching transformation can point us in the right direction and even frame a path, they, by themselves, do not change our behavior. Simply, we cannot think our way into a new way of seeing and being. Only *practice* takes us there. It's not unlike the challenge of learning to play tennis or the piano. While some understanding is required, we know that playing either tennis or piano is dependent on intentional, regular practice until new habits become internalized with ascending levels of proficiency.

It's one thing to understand the movement from a separate identity as the small self to our deeper identity as Love, beloved, being loved, and loving justly. It's another thing *to feel and live* from that shift in identity. It's the difference from *thinking* about transformation and *participating* in the process of being transformed. In the postscript of the last letter, we get a glimpse from Merton of his "waking from a dream of separateness" and the feeling of intimacy inherent in the experience of transformation.

You can relax. I have no particular practice of prayer or meditation to sell. I heed Merton's caution: "Contemplation cannot be taught. It cannot be even be clearly explained. It can only be hinted at, suggested, pointed to, symbolized. It should be one's own discipline, not a routine mechanically imposed from the outside."[1] You have your own practices, as do other readers of these letters. I only offer hints that may challenge, entice, or suggest.

During our time working together, I remember us talking about prayer. I can't recall the specifics, but I suspect we talked about this helpful distinction: In the tradition of spirituality there are two types of practices—*kataphatic* and *apophatic*. You and I grew up spiritually on kataphatic practices that call on our faculties of reason, memory, imagination, feelings, and will. These practices feature words—reading words, interpreting words with more words, singing words, and praying with words.

Consider these kataphatic practices as one frame. It's a frame we appreciate. We both cherish this tradition. I cannot imagine the practice of our faith apart from interpreting Scripture, hymns, litanies, and prayers both written and spoken. These spiritual practices have been for us bridges of transcendence, taking us to our center, our primary identity as unconditionally loved.

The reframe—or more accurately another frame to place alongside our more familiar practice—is apophatic practice, sometimes called contemplative prayer. The apophatic practice is prayer beyond words or without words. It bypasses our capacities for analytical reasoning, binary thinking, and even imagination. In one teacher's metaphor, this spiritual practice puts a stick in the spokes of our inner wheels of incessant thinking.

This transformative practice is more about subtraction than addition. Simply put, it's about becoming quiet, turning inward, letting go of thoughts and words, resting in the silence, allowing ourselves once again to be rooted and grounded in Love. As our busy mind returns with its thoughts (which it does constantly and with a vengeance), we once again relinquish their grip, falling back into the grace of being loved and loving. You keep returning to who you are at your core. *Simply* is the word I just wrote. Yes, it's simple to explain, but, as you know well, it's profoundly difficult to do.

My curiosity about apophatic or contemplative prayer began with the Trappist monk Father Louis, known to the world as Thomas Merton. From 1963–1964 I was at the right place at the right time with the right person. During post-Vatican years with the doors opening up wide in the Roman Catholic Church, Thomas Merton became friends with Glenn Hinson, a young professor at my seminary, Southern Baptist Theological Seminary. On three occasions I visited Merton with Glenn at the Abbey of Gethsemane in nearby Bardstown, Kentucky. On the third occasion Merton met with our small seminar and discussed with us my graduate paper on his teaching of mystical theology to the novices. I was drawn to Merton—not just to his thinking but more to his person, his humor, his presence. Through subsequent years my fascination remained, but only much later did I incorporate his teaching into my practice.

This "much later" was almost thirty years later in 1992, shortly before you joined our ministerial staff. Our church was in the middle of the contentious process of discerning our response to a request for a gay union (marriage), about which I wrote in a previous letter, "Agents of Change." "We have backed into a whirlwind," I heard myself saying more than once. During this four-month season of congregational discussion, church members were excited; members were exiting. Members were becoming more invested; members were disinvesting. Daily, on the phone, in letters, even in the local paper, people were voicing, "Yes! Thumbs up!" while others were declaring, "No! Thumbs down!" Telephone calls to the church office ranged from "Pass on my support" to "Pass on my disbelief/disdain/disagreement!"

How could I remain reasonably centered and grounded within this overheated situation? That was my urgent question. I turned to familiar practices, my "go-to" scriptural treasures: Psalm 139; Isaiah 40, in particular the "walking and not fainting"; the "Jesus with you" promises; Paul's "nothing, no thing, now or later, can separate us from the love of God" and his "putting on whole armor of God" when up against systemic forces. There were other dependable resources—favorite writers, music, friends, and preferred trails to walk.

During that troubled time, a gift fell "out of the blue" in the mail. It was from a distant Sunday school teacher whom I knew from my university days. He had read about our controversy in his local Nashville newspaper. This gift, a book, reopened for me the contemplative, apophatic way of praying called Centering Prayer, to which Merton had introduced me years earlier. The book was *Open Mind, Open Heart* by Father Thomas Keating. My former Sunday school teacher, John, whom I had not seen for over forty years, added this inscription on the inside title page: "Mahan, I thought this may be useful during stressful days." And it was.[2]

My reference to Keating begs me to include this telling story in which he reports the experience of a nun who was being trained in this way of praying: After trying for twenty minutes, she lamented, "Oh, Father Keating, I'm such a failure at this prayer. In twenty minutes I've had 10,000 thoughts." His quick response: "How lovely! Ten thousand opportunities to return to God." This story makes the point: returning to our identity as beloved even 10,000 times speaks to our commitment to transcend our busy mind while consenting to the action of God within. The nun, we could say, was experiencing a vigorous aerobic workout of her inner capacity to release the grip on our pressing thoughts and feelings.

There are so many options. A transformative practice can be as simple as breathing with intention. I'm fond of this story told by Franciscan Richard Rohr: A learned rabbi at a conference confronted him about the frequent misunderstanding among Christians of the second commandment—not to take God's name in vain—protesting that it has nothing to do with the prohibition of swearing. Rather, he insisted, it's a prohibition on any naming of God. God cannot be captured with words. The Mystery must be preserved and protected.

Yahweh, the Jewish reference to God, the rabbi noted, is actually a breath prayer, not a name. *Yah* is the in-breath; *weh* is the out-breath. Breathing in *Yah* as spirit and being loved; breathing out *weh* as gratitude, healing, and passion for justice. By repeating this breath prayer, you feel the *ruach*, the Hebrew word for either breath or spirit or wind breathing through you. Breathing in, breathing out.[2] In the words of Lord Tennyson, "Closer is He than breathing and nearer than hands and feet."[3]

Nancy, whatever your form of contemplative practice, it's a gentle way of quieting the anxious mind, exercising the muscle of letting go, lowering the egoic voices, and letting yourself down into the currents of being held and carried. It's falling into a Love we can never accomplish, nor do we have to.

It's the shift that matters in these different ways of contemplative praying: from analytical mind to heart that feels and sees connection; from striving to allowing; from self-consciousness to Christ-consciousness; from living for God to living from God.

My hope is that you and other pastors reading these letters will place these apophatic practices alongside the kataphatic ones we know so well. It's both/and, not either/or.

I end with a warning: Contemplative practices can become just another way the ego tries to justify itself. This inner work, as all our work, runs the risk of being an additional attempt to earn the well-being that is already ours to receive and out of which to live.

So it's tricky. Perhaps what matters is the longing to become centered as beloved, a conduit of compassion, a flute for the Music. If our deepest yearning is to live and serve from this Source, then I trust the right practices have appeared and will keep appearing.

It's practice I'm urging, not *which* practice. Current neuroscientists confirm what our contemplative heritage has known through the years: *We become what we practice.* That is the point of this letter. It took me a while to say it: The hard part is practicing.

The next reframe—ministry as spiritual practice—takes practicing transformation into your workplace.

With gratitude,
Mahan

Notes

[1] A Thomas Merton quote found on the website OctaneCreative.com, http:// octanecreative.com/merton/quotes.html

As promised, I am not promoting any method of contemplative prayer. The practice of Centering Prayer referenced in this letter is one of the many transformative practices widely explained and available today. If interested for more information, I recommend the book, *Centering Prayer and Inner Awakening* by Cynthia Bourgeault.

[2] "The Yahweh Prayer" is described in a lecture from Richard Rohr at the Drew University Soul Work Conference, November 6, 2010.

[3] These frequently quoted words affirming the intimacy of God's presence are from Lord Tennyson's short poem, "The Higher Pantheism."

Ministry as Spiritual Practice

Dear Nancy,

This letter, the last one, may be my most important one. This reframe turned my view of ministry upside down. The idea came from Ted Purcell, a friend for over forty years. You knew Ted when he was a faithful member of Pullen.

It was March 1988 on one of our Sabbath days. Ted, Mel, Alan, Anne, and I were together in deep discussion about some concern I can't recall. But in the midst of our conversation, as an off-the-cuff comment, Ted gave an observation that found no traction in the discussion. No one picked up on it, but it must have lodged somewhere in my unconscious because a few days later it resurfaced during a walk with my dog, Katie.

Ted's idea reminded me of the challenge I had once heard from family systems theorist Rabbi Edwin Friedman. Friedman proposed, "What if you treat your ministry as a *research project*?"[1]—that is, approach any aspect of it with the curious question "What can I discover and learn here?" But Ted's idea seemed to go deeper.

Ted said, "*Maybe vocation is for our transformation.*" It's the reversal that caught my attention. We would expect to hear that our vocation is for the transformation of others. But pastoral ministry as a resource for *our* transformation—well, that's another matter. His words, the order of them, intrigued me.

From that moment I began to play with the idea that our work itself could be a spiritual practice. I invite you to do the same. If transformation—the grace of receiving and living from our identity as beloved—is the journey we are on, then ministry brings ample challenges for that inner soul work. If we are committed to being transformed, whatever we experience can feed that inner movement.

This may be good news for those who find regular practices of contemplative prayer to be particularly difficult. This is a more active spiritual practice, a practicing not on the prayer cushion but "on the run." In the previous letter we looked at contemplative prayer from the apophatic tradition as a repeated practice of letting go of our busy minds and returning to our Center. In this reframe I'm exploring how *our work* itself can be the impetus for this same transformative path.

This is another angle on this reframe: Our baptism trumps our vows of ordination and marriage. At the rite of baptism, whether as infants or adults, we dramatize the affirmation: My life is not primarily about me; it's about the Christ-life living through me. Our pastoral ministry can mirror that same transformational shift: from our ministry being primarily about us to our ministry being about the More Than Us, the Music, the Christ-life living through us. We are considering that our work is the very place where that transformation can take place.

Two assumptions I want to establish before we proceed: The first is that you and I have this amazing capacity to watch ourselves. Sometimes called the "inner observer" or "witnessing presence," it's that part of us that sits back and takes in what's happening within. Right now, your inner observer may be noticing your responses to this letter. Or you may be curious about some other aspect of your behavior: Why did I react to Allen with anger? My response last night to her or him or it—what's that about? This part of you can imagine yourself where you were at 10:00 yesterday morning or where you will likely be at 10:00 tomorrow morning. It's a remarkable capability within us, to observe ourselves in action.

The second assumption follows: We can watch ourselves in action and make a choice of how to respond. Do you remember when you read *Man's Search for Meaning* by Victor Frankl? You know the story: When taken to a Nazi extermination camp, Frankl was stripped of all his external identities: his vocation, his family, his friends, his clothes, his manuscript, his hair, even his name. He discovered for himself, and for us all, that the one thing that could not be taken from him was his freedom to respond. Even in these brutal, inhuman circumstances, he claimed the choice to respond in ways that gave meaning to his suffering. This insight, along with the gift of an inner observer, makes possible our use of our work as spiritual practice.

The stance is one of welcoming. You welcome the joys, the gifts of grace. You welcome the triggers of reactive energy that evokes ego's need for control, fight, flee, or freeze. You welcome all the experiences with curiosity. All invite our response. All present us with choices.

Cynthia Bourgeault gives this practice a name: *The Welcoming Practice* is what she calls "a powerful companion for turning daily life [ministry] into a virtually limitless field for inner awakening."[2] According to Bourgeault, this practice is a three-step process. She provides an ordered way to turn what "hooks" us into opportunities for soul work.

First, she suggests we pay attention to the disorienting experiences. It might be a criticism, a threat, a failure, or even an unexpected array of compliments. Whatever the disturbance, you *focus and sink in*. You focus on the sensation in your body from the reaction being felt. Shortness of breath? Jaw clenched? Knots in your stomach? Fight or flight adrenaline rush? Burst of pleasure from affirmation? Whatever the feeling, don't try to change it. Just be present to what you are sensing in your body. Don't think or interpret. Rather, feel and locate these feelings within you.

Second, you *welcome*. This is the counterintuitive, paradoxical part. You welcome with curiosity the particular feeling and bodily sensations: "Welcome, fluttering heart"; or "Welcome, tightening chest"; or "Welcome, shortness of breath"; or "Welcome, nauseous stomach"; or "Welcome, flush of pride"; or "Welcome, muscle tightness." Welcome all "unexpected guests" with gifts to bear. In this welcoming practice you are creating an inner state of hospitality. But note this important distinction: You are not focusing on what provokes the reaction—the criticism, the adulation, the judgment, the success, the failure. Rather, you are welcoming the sensations associated with the precipitating event. You accept fully the feelings until the reaction runs its chemical course through your body, usually thirty to sixty seconds.

Then you face a decision. By observing your inner reactions, you come to a point of choice. One option is to attach to the feelings and let "the hook" take you up into ego-inflation or down into ego-deflation. In making that choice, you just added another stone to the pile of former stones of similar reactive responses. This experience of staying hooked into judging or pride or fear or defensiveness or anger has a "here we go again" feel to it. In these instances you strengthen a familiar miserable emotion.

Or you can take another step: You can *let go*. Once you have honored the sensations, feeling them in your body, then you can choose to release them. This can happen naturally as we allow the experiences to flow through us. Or you can gently but firmly say something like "I let go of my inadequacy, my pride, my fear, my shame, my judgment." After the release, and with intentionality, you then focus on something or someone else. Where you focus your attention is where your energy goes. And where your energy goes, you go.

And I add a fourth act assumed by Bourgeault. Once you release these reactive emotions, take a moment to recall and reaffirm who you are. It's the transformative shift from feeling caught up in reactivity to remembering your given identity as God's child, as compassion, as gratitude, as joy, as self-giving. Once again, you are choosing to let yourself down into the currents of grace that carry you. It's a choice, a repeated choice, a shift, a practice, a gesture of surrender.

Don't believe that I follow this practice every time these "visitors" come knocking at the door of my house! Sometimes I do. Maybe 5%, possibly 10% of the time I do. It takes time, intention, and self-discipline. But when I can catch myself, pause, watch, welcome, feel, and release, then I experience another little taste of freedom. I strengthen a degree of response-ability. I weaken a degree of re-activity.

I remind us that this spiritual practice is possible because our core is not in question. Our center is secure. Our being beloved is a given. Our identity, rooted and grounded in God's love, provides a stable platform from which to welcome and respond to the "unexpected visitors" as the many triggers keep coming our way.

In this letter I have been raising the question "What if, in addition to our work of service to the church, this very work itself becomes a fertile field in which, like seeds, our egos are broken open to the transforming forces for us?" Nancy, I hesitate to mention my unhelpful response to you when on occasion you were complaining about some irritating member. I remember saying, "Well, God provides." After you rolled your eyes, this either evoked laughter or the response "That's not helpful!" Well, not to blame it on God, but our work sure provides ample occasions to practice this welcoming practice. There will be no lack of triggers. Unwanted, disorienting "visitors" will keep knocking at our door. To see them as gifts for our maturation verges on the impossible—or, let's say, an impossible possibility.

It strikes me that we have limited control over achieving our ministry goals. But we do have the choice between uncontrolled reactions and learned responses. It's our one freedom, this freedom to respond. What if we gave the relationships we experience the power to change us? "What if," as Ted's words live on, "our vocation is for our transformation?"

With this reframe in mind, a prayer for the day might look like this:

Grant that I will allow the power in my relationships this day to change me.
Grant that the difficulties of today strengthen my capacity to let go of attachments to outcomes, to being right, and to being affirmed.
Grant that preparations for preaching and teaching bring to me a Word that breaks me open to the grace I'm privileged to declare.
Grant that I will harbor in my self-awareness these sobering reminders:

My ministry is not about me;
My ministry is not up to me;
My ministry is not about my worth.
Grant that I find in the joys and sorrows of today the gifts to be seen, named, and
lived.
Grant that the invisible presence of Christ, the very love that is God, become
visible in the challenges of this day.
Grant today the courage to bear the symbols of God, even to be a symbol of God,
without playing God.

Nancy, we have come to the end of these letters. In writing them I have been reminded frequently of our shared love for our vocation. In retirement I've watched you continue to thrive in this work. After your first year I remember a church member asking how you were doing. My answer has proven to be both perceptive and predictive. I said, "Two things about Nancy: She has good instincts for pastoral ministry, and she's eager to grow and learn."

Thank you for receiving these letters with an eye for learning and for allowing other pastors to read them over your shoulder.

With gratitude,
Mahan

Notes

[1] I am unable to find in Edwin Friedman's writing the phrase, "threat you ministry as a research project." I must have heard it in one of his lectures. No question that the phrase fits his teaching. To assume the stance of a student, thus curious about your learning is precisely included in his concept of self-differentiation. You can't be anxious and be a curious learner at the same time. At my retirement, during those in-between months after the announcement but before leaving, I framed that period as a research project, asking, sometimes with the congregation, what did we learn from our time together? What's clearer?

[2] Cynthia Bourgeault, *Centering Prayer and Inner Awakening* (Lanham, MD: Cowley Publications, 2004), 135.

Epilogue

In *Active Hope*, Johanna Macy and Chris Johnstone identify three "stories" that have emerged in our time: *business as usual* assumes our society is on the right track, fueled by a worldview of individuals essentially separate from each other and the earth, thereby competitive, comparing, and controlling; *the great unraveling* is fueled by the angst, if not despair, from experiencing the wealth gap, resource depletion, climate change, racial and ethnic divisions, war, and mass extinction of species; *the great turning* assumes a worldview of living in relationship with each other and the earth, honoring difference, knowing the joy of healing, wonder, and gratitude in the work for a more life-sustaining society.[1]

Each Sunday, you stand before a congregation living within and from these conflicting stories. And you know within yourself the claims of each one. These narratives that compete for our allegiance shed light on the tensions felt within the church and nation in our day.

Letters to Nancy springs from the root of this one conviction: Pastors are uniquely well-positioned to lead in this time of contending narratives. You have a particular version of the Story of *the great turning*, or, more accurately, the Story has you. You have the preparation. You have the experiences. You have the community. Your leadership couldn't be more timely.

In this time of dying, all the way from massive extinctions of species to the cracks, and possible crumbing, of our assumed ways of being Christian, church, and American, you know about death. You have been around dying. Others can deny death, but you cannot. You know it well, whether with persons or structures or worldviews. You bring an angle of vision, traditionally named the Paschal Mystery, that anticipates resurrection rising out of crucifixion, life rising out of death. You have seen this resurrecting power at work and proclaim regularly this possibility. And when you sense it, you align with this creative force of new creation.

In this time of disarray, you know about chaos. You know it well, whether in interpersonal relationships or congregational life or global mayhem. Regularly, you observe and experience the coming apart of what has felt stable. And you know to look for harmony emerging out of chaos. You expect to find in chaos a yearning for reordering into more wholesome, life-giving forms. You have cultivated sight for the Spirit at work in chaos. And, when discerned, you are prepared to participate in these moments of transformation, whether small or large.

In this time of insecurity and frenzy, you know about fear. Chronic anxiety is the air we all are breathing. You observe daily its predictable behaviors of blaming, reacting, polarizing—and rush toward quick fixes. Yet you know more. Regularly, you invite a grounding in grace beneath these turbulent waters. You declare our rootedness in life as beloved, as God's delight, as instruments of God's force of justice-love.

In this time when individual humans and non-human beings are seen as separate and disconnected, you see differently. Though separation appears to be the case, you know this to be an illusion. You know the *new* and *old* story of interbeing, wholeness, and the beloved community. It's old because it is the biblical story of shalom. And it's new for many people, a different way to see their world as relational through and through. Consistently you address the deep wound of our separation from each other, from God, and from the earth. You call out this lie. You name this delusion. You teach and preach "No, separation!" You keep reminding your congregation that we are loved with a Love from which no thing—now or later, in life or death—can separate us.

In this time of intense longing for certainty, you know this insistence on right believing. You have felt the force of dualistic thinking that defines others in or out. But you offer a deeper, relational knowing of the heart that's beneath tight-fisted clinging to certain ideology. Comfortable within mystery, feeling the awe of Life and Love, you are able to live with the paradox of knowing and not knowing. You keep pointing to Love's power to bless, to heal, to live through us with words that fall short every time. Daily, you bet your life and vocation on this gracious, ineffable mystery we name God, Christ, Holy Spirit, Divine, Sacred.

Granted, our current disestablishment of the church, with its status declining and its relevance questioned, seems to render as absurd the claim that your leadership is timely. Quite to the contrary, it's by leading from a sidelined, countercultural stance that so aligns you with the strongest voices in our centuries of tradition. You are well-positioned to offer the pastoral and prophetic leadership so needed in our time. With these letters I rest my case.

Mahan Siler
January 2020

Note

[1] Johanna Macy and Chris Johnson, *Active Hope* (Novato, CA: New World Library, 2012), 13–34.

CPSIA information can be obtained
at www.ICGtesting.com
Printed in the USA
BVHW040108070421
604344BV00014B/1867